TWAYNE'S WORLD AUTHORS SERIES

A Survey of the World's Literature

Sylvia E. Bowman, Indiana University
GENERAL EDITOR

DENMARK

Leif Sjöberg, State University of New York
at Stony Brook

EDITOR

H. C. Branner

(*TWAS 245*)

TWAYNE'S WORLD AUTHORS SERIES (TWAS)

The purpose of TWAS is to survey the major writers —novelists, dramatists, historians, poets, philosophers, and critics—of the nations of the world. Among the national literatures covered are those of Australia, Canada, China, Eastern Europe, France, Germany, Greece, India, Italy, Japan, Latin America, the Netherlands, New Zealand, Poland, Russia, Scandinavia, Spain, and the African nations, as well as Hebrew, Yiddish, and Latin Classical literatures. This survey is complemented by Twayne's United States Authors Series and English Authors Series.

The intent of each volume in these series is to present a critical-analytical study of the works of the writer; to include biographical and historical material that may be necessary for understanding, appreciation, and critical appraisal of the writer; and to present all material in clear, concise English—but not to vitiate the scholarly content of the work by doing so.

H. C. Branner

By T. L. MARKEY
Harvard University

Twayne Publishers, Inc.   ::   New York

Copyright © 1973 by Twayne Publishers, Inc.
All Rights Reserved

Library of Congress Catalog Card Number: 73-39779

MANUFACTURED IN THE UNITED STATES OF AMERICA

To Elias Bredsdorff

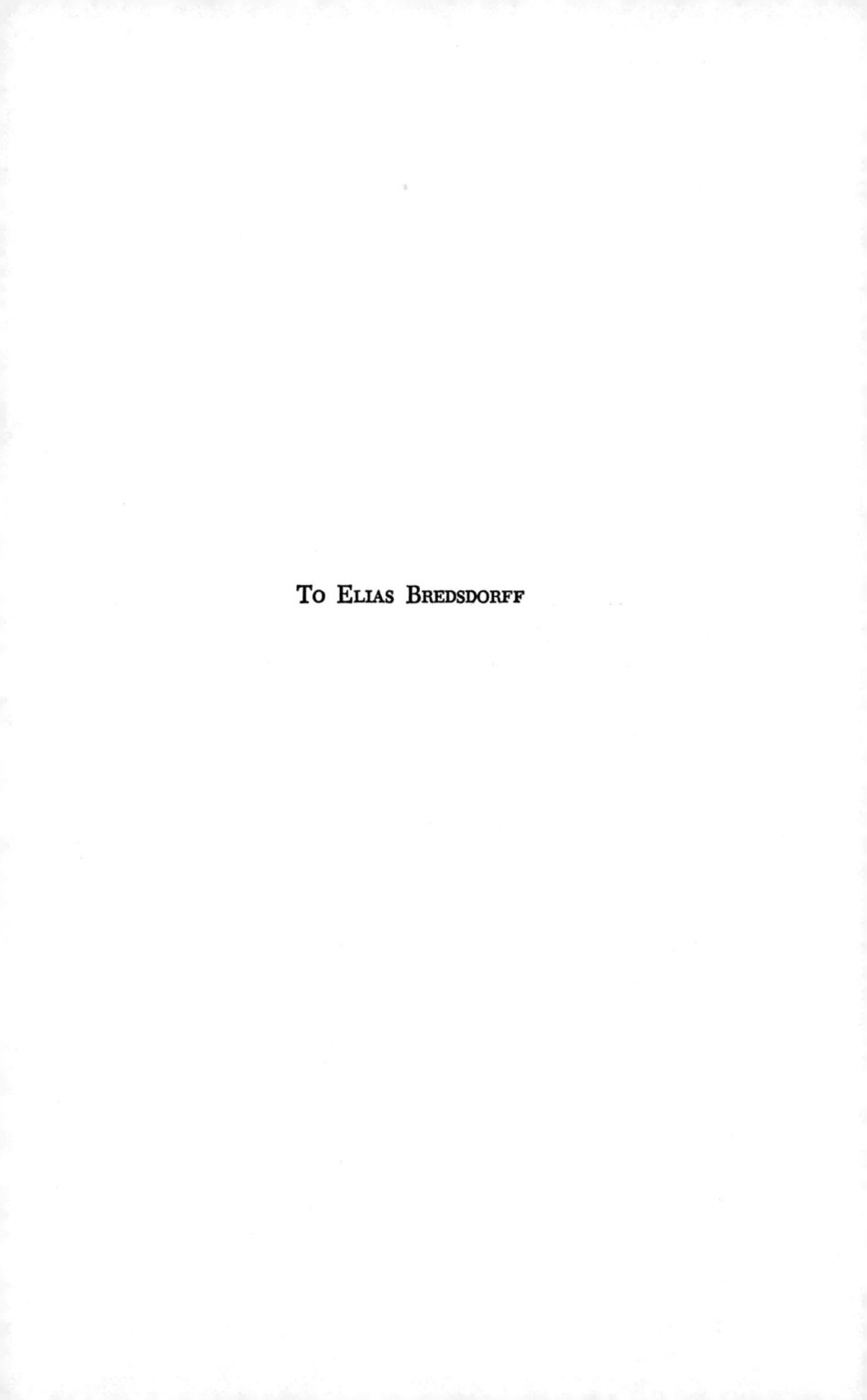

Preface

It has been my intent in the following study to give a more complete survey of the works of Hans Christian Branner (1903–1966) than has previously been given. Without doubt the finest and most introspective critiques of Branner to date are those by Jörn Vosmar and Emil Frederiksen, and I am deeply indebted to both of these works for many helpful interpretive insights. Furthermore, I have attempted to focus on the recurrence and variations of central, unifying themes in his principal works, without losing sight of the specific quality of individual texts. And beyond Branner, these themes and Branner's treatment of them indicate some of the basic issues of contemporary Scandinavian literature. As it is also the purpose of this study to introduce Branner to a larger audience, I have translated all quotes, while retaining titles in the original.

An earlier version of this study was completed while I was a Research Student at Peterhouse College, Cambridge, under the supervision of Dr. Elias Bredsdorff, Reader in Scandinavian Studies in the University of Cambridge and Fellow of Peterhouse College. I am grateful to Dr. Bredsdorff for invaluable help during the course of my work, and his intimate knowledge of Branner's works saved me from many a pitfall. I also wish to thank the Master and Fellows of Peterhouse for securing a travel grant which enabled me to assemble material on Branner at the Royal Library in Copenhagen. In Copenhagen I had the opportunity to use the *Kaas Sörensen Udklipsamling*, which includes contemporary Branner criticism and many of Branner's early short stories not subsequently republished.

Finally, I consider myself fortunate indeed to have interviewed H. C. Branner on September 7, 1965.

T. L. M.

Contents

	Preface	
	Chronology	
1.	Beginnings through *Legetöj*	13
2.	*Barnet leger ved Stranden, Drömmen om en Kvinde,* and *Historien om Börge*	35
3.	The Art of the Short Story	74
4.	Dramatic Interlude	92
5.	The End of a Phase and *Ingen kender Natten*	122
6.	Drama and Short Story once more	143
	Epilogue	157
	Notes and References	161
	Selected Bibliography	177
	Index	181

Chronology

1903   H. C. Branner born June 23 in Ordrup, a suburb of Copenhagen.
1921   Completed *studenterexamen* and entered traveling theater company.
1923   Resigned from theater company and entered publishing firm.
1930   Married Karen Moldrup on June 20.
1932   Resigned publishing position on January 1 and published first literary work, *Surdejgen* (*Sourdough*), September 4.
1936   *Legetöj* (*Toys*), first novel.
1937   *Barnet leger ved Stranden* (*The Child Playing by the Shore*).
1939   *Om lidt er vi borte* (*In a Little While We Shall Be Gone*).
1941   *Drömmen om en Kvinde* (*The Dream about a Woman*).
1942   *Historien om Börge* (*The Story of Börge*).
      Trommerne (*The Drums*).
1944   *To Minutters Stilhed* (*Two Minutes Silence*).
      Angst (*Anxiety*) appeared in the illegal anthology *Der brænder en Ild* (*A Fire Is Burning*).
1945   Translated Kafka's *The Trial*.
1946   Lectured on *Die Krise des Humanismus* (*The Crisis of Humanism*) in Germany.
1947   *Angst* (*Anxiety*), greatly revised version of earlier work with the same title.
1949   *Rytteren* (*The Riding Master*).
      Translated Kafka's *The Castle*.
      Hundrede Kroner (*A Hundred Crowns*).
1950   *The Riding Master* premièred at Stockholm's Lilla Dramaten, April 5.
1951   *Söskende* (*The Judge*) premiered in Stockholm, December 13.

At work on *Bjergene* (*The Mountains*).
1952 Fragment of *Ingen kender Natten* (*No Man Knows the Night*) appeared in *Ord och Bild* (Stockholm).
1953 *Bjergene* (*The Mountains*).
1955 *Ingen kender Natten* (*No Man Knows the Night*) appeared on December 5.
1956 *Vandring langs Floden* (*Wandering along the Tide*).
Delivered lecture, *Kunstens Uafhængighed* (*The Independence of Art*), at Danish Student Union, Copenhagen, November 24.
1958 *Thermopylæ*.
1960 *Et Spil om Kærligheden og Döden* (*A Play about Love and Death*).
1964 *Ariel*.
1965 *Mörket mellem Træerne* (*The Dark between the Trees*).
Matador, only drama written expressly for television.
1966 Died April 24 in Copenhagen.

CHAPTER 1

Beginnings through Legetöj

H. C. BRANNER was born on June 23, 1903, in Ordrup, now a suburb of Copenhagen. His childhood home—with its garden and poplars[1]—at Hyldegaards Tværvej 9 is clearly recognizable in the descriptions of childhood such as we find them in *Historien om Börge*. His father, Christian Branner, who died when Branner was five, was a headmaster, and his mother, Fanny Branner, née Frederiksen, was the daughter of H. C. Frederiksen, who founded what subsequently became Ordrup Gymnasium.

As he writes in *Glimt af mig selv*,[2] Branner had poetic aspirations even as a child:

As a little boy I lay in my bed and poetized each evening when the light had been turned out. For the most part I fabricated further on the stories I had heard about gods and kings and princesses, and about Mowgli and all his animals.[3]

After his *studenterexamen* (1921) Branner found an outlet for his aesthetic energy as an actor. As he relates in *Glimt af mig selv*, he went to Peter Jerndorff, director of the Royal Theater's School of Drama from 1886 to 1923, and read Ibsen's *Terje Vigen* aloud and was subsequently enrolled as a student. Having spent some time at the school, he was advised by Peter Nielsen, then the Royal Theater's stage director, to do a stint with a stage company on tour in the provinces. He got an engagement with, among others, Otto Jacobsens Selskab. Once on tour, he played Sören Torp and Mads in Jens Christian Hostrup's *Genboerne* and in 1922 Gustave in Dumas's *Kameliadamen*. His role as Gustave ended in fiasco after which Branner decided that he no longer wanted to be an actor, and he certainly did not want to be an author, but rather "something proper." In 1923 he entered the publishing firm of V. Pio, which became Jespersen and Pio in

13

1927; there he remained until he resigned his post on January 1, 1932. While still in the publishing business, he married Karen Moldrup on June 20, 1930. In *Glimt af mig selv* he comments on one effect of his marriage:

> Being married can mean discovering who one is—one finds one's self in a creature of the opposite sex. And I saw to my horror that it wasn't me at all who went about in white overalls. While the office man fought to gain a foothold on reality, the dreamer had tirelessly constructed his own inner reality. I hadn't written a line, but I had enough unwritten novels for the next ten years. . . . I attempted to write a book in my spare time: it became distended and drowned in rough drafts and sketches. There wasn't enough time, enough quiet. I became restless, irritable and unsociable.[4]

And so, having resigned his position with Jespersen and Pio, he embarked upon a new career as an author. In a letter to Holger Kristiansen (7/3/1937) he describes his early years as follows:

> In 1932 it became too involved for me. I broke away and embarked upon the daring venture to live by my pen. The first years were difficult enough, and essentially I still must make a living from translating.[5]

Finally, nine months after having resigned from Jespersen and Pio, his first short story was accepted by *Hjemmets Söndag*, and he made his debut in that Sunday magazine with the story *Surdejgen,* on September 4, 1932. At the time he and his wife were living on an estate in Northern Sjælland, where Branner was a private tutor.

Surdejgen[6] is the anecdotal relation by a young journalist of his meeting with a would-be playwright, Johan Sebastian Ankerstjerne, a prominent diplomat who has written a play, *Peace on Earth*. He tells the journalist that, as a schoolboy, he had written an essay criticizing his school. When he had read a rough draft of it aloud to his classmates, they had proclaimed him a hero of reform. The essay won third prize in a school competition, but when the headmaster read it aloud to the school, its satirical tone made it a good joke. Thereafter, Ankerstjerne was deposed in the eyes of his classmates. His present reaction to the misunderstood interpretation of his play is therefore rooted in a childhood experience —Branner's theme of the child in man thus comes forth in his very first story. Ankerstjerne's tragedy is that he was out of step with his times, for "he should have been born in the generation before World War I when one still believed that the face of the earth could be changed by a play."[7]

In his next story, *Prometheus*,[8] Branner again takes up the theme of an individual's inner conflict with a "concept." After the funeral of her poet husband, Martin Börner, Jonna discovers and reads three letters which her husband had received from his mistresses. Although she had been aware of her husband's infidelity, she had not known the childish form it had taken.[9] Here it is important to note the earliest occurrence of the Branneresque theme that women are often considered stronger than men, and this is brought out when Jonna says that she consoled Martin like a child.[10]

During his second year as an author, Branner enjoyed further success with the presentation of a radio play, *Eftermæle* (*Epitaph*), which won second prize in a nationwide contest conducted by the Danish State Radio, and the publication of five short stories. The first of these, *Isaksen*,[11] undoubtedly draws on Branner's personal experiences in publishing firms. In the person from whom the story takes its name we meet a character who partially resembles Halvorsen and partially Ingolf Trane in *Legetöj*. Isaksen embodies aspects of the fool figure Halvorsen and the static, formal simplicity of Trane. The story's narrator is roughly comparable to Martin Lind in *Legetöj*, and Feddersen closely resembles the coldly calculating, pike-eyed Feddersen in the same novel. The story's central incident is the plot to remove Isaksen from Bolbjerg's Stationery Company and, once he is fired, his mental collapse.

To Minutters Stilhed[12] is an acerbic social commentary à la Sinclair Lewis about the overly socially pretentious Valdemar Skjold-Lassen and his long-suffering wife, Ragna, and how they attempt to attain and keep a social position far beyond their financial means. Once the impression of apparent success has been made, and the author has skillfully controlled our sympathy so that we respect Ragna for her talent in maintaining appearances, then the narrator intrudes to tell us that all is a lie:

Shhh, this is gossip which one can actually only read in an afternoon paper, but let it be kept between us: Skjold-Lassen, who calls himself a wholesale-dealer, is not a wholesale dealer. He is a representative, an agent, if you please. Certainly in the Yellow Pages one finds under Winterfeld and Sons: extension 15: wholesale dealer V. Skjold-Lassen. However, that's only the empty title he was most graciously permitted to retain after Winterfeld swallowed him up along with his little import company due to the unpaid balance on a note.[13]

Thus, in a superb example of unreliable narrative, Branner exposes the tragedy behind the appearance of success. The intrusion has the effect of truncating credibility. Nevertheless, as the impression of success has been made with such seeming reliability, and as our empathy has been directed to Ragna who has done everything to uphold that impression, the revelation of the truth turns Ragna into a tragic figure. The truncation of credibility to convey tragic irony was a common enough device in Danish social satire during the thirties, and Branner's near contemporary, Hans Scherfig, was a master of this device.[14] Consider, for example, the following passage in Scherfig's *Det forsömte Foraar* (1940):

His mother lives in a rather large apartment in the East Station area. She was divorced from her husband when her son was a little boy in sailor's middy and knickers. And she kept the son. She has him yet. And she watches out for him and protects him from all evil influences. She watches over his health and welfare with touching care. And now you must eat, and now you must rest, and I've put out clean underwear and hankies for you.[15]

Though there are many similarities between Branner's and Scherfig's satirical writing, Branner does not have the rapid, paratactic run-on, and he never delivers the swift, poisonous jabs that are Scherfig's forte. The tragic conclusions, such as Ragna's death in *To Minutters Stilhed*, with which he sometimes closes his social satires, permit Branner's social statements to end in bitter irony which stings the reader into an awareness of the vacuity of social prestige. This is the effect of the ending of *To Minutters Stilhed*, where Skjold-Lassen, despite the loss of his wife, continues to play the game of appearances:

The sight of his friend once again released tears from wholesale dealer Skjold-Lassen. Indeed, that was the great magnate, Troch, the stern, ingenious master of Troch Textiles with ten million in shares—

Beginnings through Legetöj

and he just didn't hesitate. . . . It came so naturally that Mr. Skjold-Lassen went forth a moment and laid his head on his shoulder. "Oh, director Troch, you have no idea how glad I am that you're the first person I meet after . . . after . . . Ragna . . . ." [16]

Realistically Valdemar's reaction is ludicrous, but in his terms it is the only one possible. What begins as a satire embedded in plot and character, as in traditional high comedy, ends as a criticism of a way of life. The tragic irony of the story is expressed in the contrast between the tragic rationale of the actual situation and Valdemar's absurdity. Branner was to employ this same balance of contrasts in *Legetöj,* and *To Minutters Stilhed* is thus a preparatory exercise.

Barely two and a half months after the publication of *To Minutters Stilhed,* Branner's second radio play, *Eftermæle,* was broadcast. It received fairly favorable reviews in both *Lytteren* and *Berlingske Tidende.* The reviewer in *Berlingske Tidende* complained that:

Not once had the author tried to employ the radio's distinctive devices or possibilities.

He concluded with the following evaluation:

And through the characters' views of the dead, a series of portraits come forth by themselves—often sad and degrading, often comic and petty, but human just the same, so human that the play came to life, despite the fact that there was no real action in it.

Eftermæle[17] lies firmly within the naturalistic tradition of the Ibsenesque chamber play, and though it is certainly not a striking drama to say the least, it is important to review it in some detail, as it contains the seeds of *Barnet leger ved Stranden* (1937). Scene One opens on the funeral dinner at the home of Valdemar Hermansen, whose wife has just been buried. The guests, and in particular Dr. Einar Wahl, all praised the memory of Cæcilie Hermansen. Scene Two takes place in Dr. Wahl's bedroom. He is the robust provincial doctor, the forerunner of Dr. Torsteinson in *Barnet leger ved Stranden.* His wife tells him that Cæcilie had once posed in the nude for the noted sculptor Hans Egge who is the forerunner of his namesake in *Barnet leger ved Stranden.* Dr.

Wahl's wife is a pragmatic family manager and, as such, the forerunner of Torsteinson's wife. Wahl's robust, somewhat blasé approach to life comes out with a few deft strokes:

> Wait just a moment before telling it. It shall be enjoyed in prone position (stretches himself in the bed). Ah,—that was good! Now we shall have a little gossip.[18]

This is the sort of replique we might expect from Torsteinson. In addition to having been a model for him, Wahl's wife continues, Cæcilie also apparently carried on an affair with Egge while her husband was away. Hermansen discovered this when he returned and punished his wife severely. Thereafter she suffered a nervous breakdown, thought the devil was coming to take her soul, ran away into the night and apparently tried to drown herself.[19] Once she was rescued, she contracted pneumonia which was a contributing factor to her death. Scene Three takes place in the home of Pastor Thamsen, whose wife is Cæcilie's sister. Pastor Thamsen and his wife, Thea, together with her brother, Christian Boje,[20] discuss the causes of Cæcilie's death and condemn her for neglecting her children and her husband. The Thamsens turned Cæcilie away when she had come to them for help after Hermansen had discovered her affair with Egge and beaten her. In Scene Four we get a glimpse of Hans Egge and his model, Rigmor. They, too, discuss Cæcilie and her tragedy. Egge blames the narrowness and provincialism of the little town and its gossip for having been factors in Cæcilie's death, and he blames Hermansen as well. Asked why Cæcilie had not left Hermansen for him, Hans Egge replies:

> That's precisely what was wrong. One isn't secure when one isn't happy. Happiness, that's something which is rationed out in drops, just like medicine. And if you take it yourself, then God help you. Therefore she lacked security. She first found it again after she was beaten and had become unhappy.[21]

Egge the sensualist believes that security neurosis was the source of Cæcilie's conflict. He stresses the value of suffering and humility in preserving one's vision of life. Cæcilie was unhappy when she was secure, or should have been secure in Valdemar's sterile prison, and she was happy only when she was insecure in Egge's temple to the libido. She could only be released from the tyranny of this conflict by death.

The fifth scene takes place in the Hermansen house between Otto Hermansen, Valdemar's son and spiritual likeness, and his middle-brow wife Asta, who coldly calculates just how much money they may expect as a result of Cæcilie's death. Otto is revealed as lacking any sense of loss at his mother's death, and the scene closes as both he and Asta hear Ejvind Hermansen, Otto's younger brother, playing the piano in the living room below. Part One of the sixth scene takes place between Gudrun Clausen, Valdemar's housekeeper, and Valdemar, who has entered Gudrun's bedroom. Gudrun serves merely to permit Valdemar to answer for his treatment of Cæcilie. He says that he had no other option left open to him than the one he took: he forcefully reprimanded his wife for her affair with Egge, for her lack of responsibility toward his sons and her mismanagement of the house. Valdemar fumblingly renews his halfhearted proposal to Gudrun which she rebuffs with a sort of cockney spirit of aloofness and practical independence. At the close of this scene both hear Ejvind playing the piano, and he is at first mistaken for Cæcilie's ghost. The sins of the father are visited on the son and the father as the ghost of Cæcilie. Ejvind is symbolically attempting to recapture the spirit of sensual happiness denied his mother. In Part Two of Scene Six the play closes as Valdemar goes to his son and forcefully makes him cease his futile attempt to be spiritually one with his mother.

Eftermæle, tightly structured as it is, reminds one of Lillian Hellman's dramatic technique. Its conflict between sterility and sensuality conveys the same message as many of Eugene O'Neill's plays, such as *Desire Under the Elms;* but it is most indebted to Ibsen and the confines of his chamber plays with their condemnation of the closure of channels of communication between people and their relations to life. Cæcilie's tragedy is, in effect, that of Ibsen's Brand: the inability to command unity, not partiality, of action in the face of internal conflict. In the final analysis *Eftermæle* is a "well-made" play, but it is pretty thin soup dramatically and does not whet the appetite for more.

Drömmeren (published in *Magasinet*, October 1, 1933) is a thinly disguised semi-autobiographical short story about a poet, Magnus Klein, who meets a journalist late one evening in a café.

Klein feels that his newly found companion is ridiculing him by calling him a "dreamer." The poet then explains why the nickname "dreamer" is the most painful he knows. The autobiographical elements of *Drömmeren* are clear when we note that, as Branner writes in *Glimt af mig selv*,[22] he was called "the dreamer" by the girls in his class.

In the same year (1933) Branner also published two short stories, *Festern* and *Flöjtspilleren*, in the column *Tusind og een aften*, in *Berlingske Aftenavis*.[23] In the following year (1934) Branner again shows himself experimenting and polishing his style to express the major themes he wished to take up. The themes are social commentary in *Oluf Höegs Skæbne*, satire in *Bogholder Mortensen og Greta Garbo*, an excursus to Branner's serious work, and a disarmingly charming and realistic sketch of childhood in *Et Barn og en Mus*.

The motif of *Oluf Höegs Skæbne*[24] is again taken from the milieu of the business world and has precisely the same plot as the earlier story *Isaksen*, namely, the attempt to dislodge an elderly and ineffective employee from his seemingly secure position in a business office. Oluf Höeg, another precursor of Ingolf Trane in *Legetöj*, is a good-natured alcoholic and the victim of a carefully contrived plot.

In *Et Barn og en Mus*[25] we meet Börge, his mother, and Gokke, the maid, all of whom appear later in *Historien om Börge* (1942). Börge is a lonely, only child, shy of adults, but completely innocent in his trust of them, and most secure when alone in his attic.

> Börge himself had no lost paradise to look into. He didn't even know what innocence was and derived no pleasure in always scuffing the ground with his feet.[26]

Branner then tells us Börge's speculations on the meaning of death, while Börge reflects on memories of his grandfather's funeral. As his mother and Gokke have fabricated a death myth for him, death is something harmless:

> Besides, grandfather wasn't really dead. He was just on a visit to God and would come back sometime. Both Mother and Gokke had said that.[27]

Beginnings through Legetöj

As Börge completely trusts them, for he has never been given any reason for questioning that trust, he believes their fantastic death myth. In his lonely world, Börge makes friends with a mouse, and in his trusting innocence he confides the existence of his closest friend to Gokke. The mouse is promptly destroyed. Given the solace of the death myth, Börge believes that his friend the mouse is only sleeping and will come back to life. The mouse is placed in a box by the tile stove, and Börge is told that it will be well the next morning. The next morning the mouse is disposed of, and Börge's mother lies to him, telling him that the mouse left and told her to tell Börge never to play in the attic again. Börge sees through the lie, finds the dead mouse in the garbage can, and discovers the meaning of death. The credibility of the death myth has evaporated in a loss of confidence in parental trust. In *Et Barn og en Mus,* then, the themes of the meaning of death and the loss of innocence have been subtly unified to complement each other in showing that loss of trust may result in loss of innocence. *Et Barn og en Mus* crystallizes a seemingly insignificant experience and gives it meaning. For Börge it is the meaning of death and its accompanying sense of anxiety. Börge, a shy and overly sensitive child, can but flee from an adult view of life and death after his brutal awakening to the reality of these concepts. It is, as Anne-Katrine Gudme suggests, "at this point that almost all of Branner's gallery of weak men have come into existence." [28]

One of the most effective stylistic devices in *Et Barn og en Mus* is Branner's use of direct run-on to depersonalize Börge and mold him into a universal representative of a child:

> There are experiences which are so overwhelming that one must keep them at a distance to become clear about what has really happened. First in the evening in bed it became clear to him. He had whistled, and Peter had come and sat in front of him and looked up at him. Then he had stretched out his hand with a piece of pastry, and Peter had jumped up into his hand and eaten the pastry. Peter was a tame mouse.[29]

In the first two clauses we are given a general observation, which is then specifically related to Börge via a piece of narrative connective ("first in the evening. . . ."), which connects the general observation with Börge's thoughts. The latter are then given in the form of paratactic coordinations with the conjunction *and*, to reproduce the breathless, disjunctive narrative of children. The direct run-on of introductory general observation, connective, and Börge's own thoughts effectively relates Börge to a general insight and thereby transforms him into a general representative.[30]

Bogholder Mortensen og Greta Garbo[31] is a fine piece of comedy, a sort of comedy of humors, and one of the few Branner ever wrote. A fat, middle-aged bookkeeper falls in love with his unobtainable dream of a woman, Greta Garbo. This is a jewel of a comic short story and a fine reworking of a somewhat hackneyed theme. As related by Jörn Vosmar,[32] Branner was accused by Julius Bomholt, the literary historian and novelist, of having plagiarized this story from Josef Maria Frank's novel, *Den Mand, der elsker Greta Garbo*. Branner replied that he had neither read nor heard of Frank's book.

Recently a fragment, *Hans Majestæt*, which is possibly from 1934, has been published for the first time in *Gyldendals Julebog*.[33] It is a deeply personal piece in which Branner asserts that the mind of the child and the clarity of a child's vision are necessary prerequisites for an author:

Give me your eyes with which to see, give me your hands with which to create.—Give me a scrap of your childhood, little king, and there shall never be thoughts which do not find their form.[34]

In 1935 Branner published only three short stories: *Hvad er Sandhed?*, *Sjukos Sjæl*, and *Hannibals Træsko*.[35] Sjuko, gift of a wealthy landowner, is the pet dog in an old lady's home. He has been petted, pampered, fawned over, and stuffed with cream cakes by the love-starved ladies until he becomes one of those unfortunate few to have actually been killed by kindness. Their reaction to Sjuko's death exposes them variously as petty, self-centered, or downright cruel, but essentially as emotionally poverty stricken and starved for human contact.

The story *Hannibals Træsko*[36] is told in the first person by Hannibal's former classmate who, now relating the tale from the vantage point of adulthood, was sympathetic toward the proletarian Hannibal's feeble efforts for social acceptance and the catastrophic form they finally took: expulsion from the school. The "I"

Beginnings through Legetöj

of the story took no part in Hannibal's conflict, because he was a dreamer, one who could not accept social responsibility even on an infantile level. Here again Branner presents the theme of the weak, ineffectual person in conflict with a stronger, more decisive character and the failure of the former to assert himself.

In 1936 Branner's first novel, *Legetöj*, appeared, and in the same year he also published three short stories. In the interests of continuity we shall discuss these three stories before turning to the novel.

Lördag Aften[37] marks a significant stylistic departure from Branner's other short stories. It is a simultaneous telling of two stories: one of a young author, Martin, and one of a young worker, Karl, who have both lied that they have been successful. The parallel is drawn very neatly: Martin and his wife can rationalize the necessity of the lie of life, while Karl and his fiancée are barely aware of its existence.

Lördag Aften is, as Branner interjects, the story of "small bitter victories and small bitter defeats"[38] which control the fate of the little man. The device of parallel narration, of splicing Martin's and Karl's stories together, gives the impression of simultaneity and permits recognition of the relatedness of their conflicts, no matter how different they are as individuals. The splicing unites Karl and Martin as brothers in the same way as Simon and Tomas are united as brothers in *Ingen kender Natten,* and this story is the first instance of the splicing technique Branner was to employ in that novel, as well as in *Drömmen om en Kvinde.*

The conceptual cement of *Lördag Aften* is compounded of love and anxiety. Anxiety takes the form of a flight from reality, just as it does in *Drömmeren, Et Barn og en Mus,* and *Iris*. The joy generated by the "lie of life" has cheered Martin's heart and renewed his love for his wife, and he sees her in everything as he passes through the city on a Saturday evening. Anne-Katrine Gudme has summed up the impact of this story in the following way:

> . . . between the impressions he registers, between the humdrum stories he snaps up in passing, there are many that run transversely to his frame of mind. They are like grains of sand of something gone wrong which are barely perceived: one notes an undercurrent of anxiety, which—without one's being able to realize it yet—is an echo of the protagonist's own situation. This impression is strengthened during Martin and Hanne's exhilarating celebration; bluffing is noted behind

the playfulness, the quick leaps over a suppressed knowledge of something.[39]

Tre Mænd vender hjem tells of a salesman's return home to Copenhagen from a trip to Germany. It is an impressionistic pastiche which consists of reflections on a train. The reflections are punctuated by the repetitive use of onomatopoeia, which reproduces the sound of a train in a manner strongly reminiscent of Thomas Wolfe. The disjunctive note sounded by his reflections is echoed by the steady *dak-dak-dak* of the train as he gropes in search of solutions to the problems in his personal life and the world about him:

—why can't people ever work together without hate and envy. As if conditions in the outside world weren't bad enough. Who says there'll be anything at all to do in Germany next year, what then? And if there's war—that's what Rohde thought—[40]

Power, prestige, personal desperation and anxiety, as well as the necessity to maintain appearances for the sake of appearances, are, of course, the major themes of *Legetöj*, and this story is but a brief listing of those themes in concentrated form.

Iris[41] is another story of childhood in which an only child of older parents finds herself ostracized from her classmates. At the outset we are introduced to another potential Iris, Margrete, who has also been ostracized from the exclusive inner circle of Alice and her confidante, Ruth. Unlike Iris, Margrete has calmly accepted ostracism and has resigned herself to the role of "fat" Margrete; but she, too, is clever. When Alice befriends Iris, a whole new world opens for Iris, for at last she has been admitted to the inner circle. But Alice, too, has just been ostracized from the inner circle Iris hoped she had finally entered, and Alice has merely fallen back on Iris as the only friend she can hope to acquire. Her friendship is nothing more than a one-sided acquisition of someone to help her. But all this—Iris's loneliness, ostracism, and final acceptance—is merely background for the story's central incident: Iris's defense of Alice. The teacher discovers that Alice has been copying Iris's homework, and, in order to save her friend and her friendship, Iris lies and says that she has copied from Alice. The lie is discovered and the friendship evaporates. Afterward Iris,

Beginnings through Legetöj

like the poet in *Drömmeren* and the playwright in *Surdejgen*, retreats from reality. She becomes sick and finally returns to school to discover that Margrete has replaced her as Alice's friend. The story's pattern is clearly that of an hourglass, for in the course of the story Iris and Margrete have exchanged places. This pattern shows how easily Margrete replaced Iris and thereby the source of Iris's anxiety.

Our discussion of *Iris* concludes our survey of Branner's writings up to the publication of his first novel, *Legetöj*. We should pause here to summarize various aspects of the works reviewed so far. From our survey of the fifteen short stories,[42] the one radio play and the lyrical fragment *Hans Majestæt*, we may conclude that, during his first four years as a published author, Branner was constantly experimenting with new techniques while constructing a poetic world replete with its own distinctive themes and motifs. He began as a journalistic reporter, a photographer and narrator of the brief episode, as is shown by the style and manner of *Surdejgen*, *Prometheus*, and *Drömmeren*. In *Isaksen*, *To Minutters Stilhed*, *Oluf Höegs Skæbne*, and *Tre Mænd vender hjem* he attempted to convey a panoramic view and offer a diagnosis of a society considered sick to the core in its fight for trivial prestige and power with no larger humanitarian ends in view. In *To Minutters Stilhed* and *Bogholder Mortensen og Greta Garbo* he showed himself to be a social satirist and that he, like his near contemporary Hans Scherfig, could make biting commentaries on the cancerous fantasies of his time: the dream of prestige and the dream of erotic surrogates.

The key to his success as a short-story writer was his ability to rapidly uncover the critical conflicts in human relations. This was a result of his ability to see behind the façade of human encounters and expose the secrets we so often withhold from one another. When asked what his leading motifs were, Branner made the following statements in an enlightening interview in *Politiken* (November 23, 1941):

> It's difficult to say what I'm interested in without being banal, but perhaps I can say it in this way. There are things which people hide from one another. I note them. By way of example I can mention that when I listen to a conversation it's not what's said that interests me, but what lies behind; why those in question express themselves in a

particular way. Everyone lies and boasts, and it's up to me to find out the hidden motives.

The conflicts he depicts usually engender an abiding feeling of personal anxiety in the protagonist. It is the feeling of anxiety which creates the inner tension in the best of his short stories and permits them to expose the depths of human experience. It is the anxiety of a school girl who finds herself ostracized by her classmates. It is the anxiety of a young boy as he attempts to comprehend the meaning of death and confronts the demythologized reality of the adult world. It is the anxiety of a group of elderly ladies who find themselves spiritually dead and their lives emotionally hollow. Time and again the individual is faced with a situation in which he confronts an experience, or a conflict, or a concept which he cannot resolve. "I am," Branner once said, "chiefly interested in human situations, and it is the psychological impact of the situation which determines character.[43] In his failure to resolve his personal conflict, his crisis, the individual is overcome by anxiety, and he flees from reality, just as Iris, Börge and the "dreamer-poet" all flee. Martin, the author in *Lördag Aften,* is caught up in a typical Branneresque situation. Faced with the frustrations of failure and filled with anxiety in his frustration, he retreats from reality and composes a lie. A retreat to the seeming security of fantasy was obviously one of Branner's own traits, as he says in *Dæmoner ved Daggry*:

> Something had happened in my childhood which had alienated me from reality—not something awful or merely unusual, not something quite ordinary which certainly happens for many children. No one is responsible for it, and I myself almost never think about it anymore, not now when I'm alone with it. But something happened which alienated me from real life. I didn't dare live it. I had to poetize it and dream it.[44]

Often, as we have seen, Branner tries to recreate that initial childhood experience which makes reality alien to one's nature, or, more often, he shows how a childhood experience can lead to arrested development in adulthood. This is the source of Branner's child in man theme.[45] The Branneresque dreamer often finds his liberation, his guide back to reality and the resolution of his conflict in the form of a woman. It is the strong woman—and Bran-

Beginnings through Legetöj

ner's women are usually stronger and have greater depths of character than do his male protagonists—who has the power to release the forces of love and understanding which rescue man from the brink of emotional despair.[46] It is a woman with strength of character and incisive intuition who punctures Martin's lie and gives him the strength to continue in his struggle.

In the interview in *Politiken*[47] Branner commented as follows on his interest in the short story:

> ... yes, the novella interests me very much. First because there was money in it, then there was the purely artistic interest, but it's a difficult genre. Often it doesn't succeed and often it takes a long time.

Having established himself as a short-story writer and conducted stylistic experiments with some basic themes in those stories, Branner then set out to write a novel in which:

> I had wanted to show how people's struggle for power permeates the whole of society and destroys working conditions for the individual. ... For most people work is just a springboard for vanity, ambition, and striving.[48]

The form which Branner selected to convey this message was that of the collective novel, the most dominant prose genre in Danish literature from the late twenties through the early forties. As such, *Legetöj* is written in much the same manner as other similar novels of the era, such as: Hans Kirk's *Fiskerne* (1928) and *Daglejerne* (1936), Leck Fischer's *Kontormennesker* (1933), Harald Herdal's *Man skal jo leve* (1934) and, with its deft strokes of satire, Hans Scherfig's *De forsömte Foraar* (1940). The collective novelists of the thirties saw, as Ole Hyltoft Petersen astutely notes:

> ... that modern society, the metropolis, the factory, the office, the union, and science functioned with the power of cooperation. It was the collectives which were developmentally and culturally formative. It had become the task of literature to show the individual in his social interdependence. The searchlight was turned from the individual to the group. It demanded breadth of presentation which only the novel could offer.[49]

By giving serialized descriptions of the reactions of various characters to a central phenomenon, the collective novel permits the reader to make a causal connection between group attitudes and problems and individual outlooks on life. The reader "feels" individually and "understands" collectively. In view of these facts, it seems only natural that, once he had established himself as a short-story writer, Branner chose the collective novel as the form for his first novel.

Legetøj is the story of a state within a state, the state of the Kejser toy company, and of the lives of those who work there. It may be read and interpreted on several levels: as the story of a business enterprise, or of how the splintered mind of a young man, Martin Lind, matures and unifies, or as a description of a power struggle in a microcosm in which an idealized version of reality is contrasted with reality as it reveals itself.[50]

The state of Kejser stores is ruled by Herman Kejser, who regards himself as a latter-day Napoleonic commander of a commercial empire.[51] The office at Kejser stores houses the bourgeoisie; its secretaries, the dissipate Ingolf Trane, and the firm's would-be dictator, Johan Feddersen. In his incessant struggle for power and prestige, Feddersen is repeatedly described as "the evil man," "the servant of the dark" and "the pike." The proletariat, Bauer, Avnsöe, and Skovman, work in the packing department in the cellar. Feddersen's purpose in this microcosm is to drive the workers to greater effectivity so that he may enhance his own prestige. To accomplish this he resorts to terror tactics. In the world of Kejser stores there is only one goal: advancement upward from the proletariat in a quest for power and prestige. In such a society the weak and insecure become easy prey to Feddersen's terror tactics when he holds out the only possibility of advancement. Only two members of the society remain impervious to Feddersen's tactics: Ditmarc, the firm's buyer, and Karl Svendsen, its chauffeur. Feddersen attempts to blackmail Ditmarc for his underhanded dealings with Wollertsen, the carpenter, but he is finally outwitted. He also fails in his personal life, as his tyranny over his wife drives her to insanity, flight, and finally death, and it also results in the death of his daughter.

The distinctly unhealthy society of Kejser stores is rotten and debt-ridden. Its quarters are not the fine building the façade seems to indicate, for the beams are rotten and paint is peeling

Beginnings through Legetöj

from the walls. The firm's supposedly distinguished traditions are nonexistent. Its venerable trade license, reputedly yellow with age, is actually tarnished by coffee stains. The wares sold by the company are fraudulent copies of better quality goods. Their colors fade in the sun. Gold and silver surfaces peel off to reveal a core of lead. Under the veneer of acceptable appearances there seethes a cauldron of falsehood, petty intrigues, and ineptitude.

In the midst of this sick milieu we find two healthy characters: Martin Lind and Klara Kvistgaard. Martin Lind is an outsider, the son of a successful man and has been apprenticed to Kejser stores. He is weak and pliable, but at the outset he attempts to follow the rules and achieve the purposeless goals of power and prestige within the firm. Nevertheless, he has enough insight to see the fatuity of the goals and warped ethics of his milieu. He is caught in the dilemma of whether or not to play the role his milieu demands or to opt out. Weak and indecisive as he is, he is transformed into a resourceful and purposeful being through the agency of Klara, the young office girl with whom he falls in love.

The splintered, indecisive mind of Martin Lind, a sort of *interbellum* Hamlet, unifies and matures, enabling him to pass judgment on the society surrounding him. Disappearing behind the mask of Martin Lind's *alter ego* and thereby permitting an inner monologue to take place between the two, Branner has Martin lay bare *Legetöj*'s central thesis:

Go your own way, said the face in there, save yourself in time.—Yes, but my future, my entire career. The face sneered. A word for power. —One cannot take a leap into the dark. One must hold onto the permanent things one has.—The only permanent thing in the world is a person's ethical worth.—[52]

The contingency of his inner conflict and its gradual enfolding have prepared us for the statement of this postulate, and, as Emil Frederiksen asserts:

And among the novels of the 1930s which have survived H. C. Branner's *Legetöj* is the only one which has the courage to advance such a naked, pointed moralizing formula as this.[53]

Though Martin Lind opts out of the power politics and demoralizingly tyrannical realm of Kejser stores, the firm itself and the values it represents goes on. Kejser stores are headed toward financial ruin, but the night before the firm is to be dissolved, fire breaks out. Prudently, just before the fire, Feddersen has increased the fire insurance, and the firm can therefore continue—this time with Feddersen as co-director.

Legetöj is divided into three sections which are assigned themes: 1) traditions, 2) prestige, and 3) power, each section being prefaced with a short introduction in which that section's theme is developed. In the first section Herman Kejser comments on the firm's traditions, but we soon learn that those traditions are either worthless or nonexistent. The prefaces to the other two sections clearly point out the microcosmic nature of *Legetöj*'s milieu and unite its atmosphere with the spirit of the era in which it was written.

These prefaces programmatically relate *Legetöj*'s message: traditions, when uncritically examined and blindly accepted, assume power and prestige and thereby power. The prefaces also relate the world of Kejser stores to the world beyond and turn *Legetöj* into an allegory: the world of Kejser stores is Denmark under the threat of Nazi Germany. Herman Kejser represents the impoverished idealism of the old order, and Feddersen is a would-be Nazi dictator. By opening *Legetöj* to an allegorical interpretation Branner has availed himself of a means of commenting on the social ills of the time, and he effectively indicates that one of the chief causes of those ills is arrested development. Terror tactics are the ploys of recalcitrant children who can assert themselves only by forcefully imposing their wills upon others. National Socialism is the product of arrested development. In *Legetöj* this assertion is less explicit than implicit, because the theme of arrested development is often communicated by symbols, similes, and extended metaphors. A perpetual repetition of similes: like on a child, a playing child, etc.,[54] in many of which *play* and *child* are united, shows that the inhabitants of Kejser stores are adults who have been frozen as prepubescent children in the maturation process.

The suggestion that the adult is a child is reenforced by constant reference to the idea that adults play childish games. The capital for Kejser stores came from profits made from the games of childish adults. Vilhelm Kaiser played with his family name and changed it to Kejser. Martin Lind pretends that his bike is a

Beginnings through Legetöj

car.[55] Herman Kejser plays a game of assembling pornographic literature and pretends that he is Napoleon.[56] Ingolf Trane pretends that he is still a captain in the cavalry. He carries a riding crop, secretly dons his old uniform, and plans the office activities along the lines of military games. Feddersen pretends that he is an aristocrat while attending meetings of the militant Order of the Seven Swords. For all three, Herman, Trane and Feddersen, their military pretensions are surrogates for a lack of masculinity. Their militant games metaphorically relate the world of Kejser stores to the police state, and, as they are the activities of childish adults, they reduce militancy to child's play. Jelva Feddersen sleeps with a doll. Henry Avnsöe pretends that he is a cowboy while he watches a western taken directly from "an adult's childhood." Finally, even emotional relationships which obtain between various characters are viewed as games. Herman Kejser believes that Martin Lind's love for Klara is nothing more than a game. As he is himself incapable of mature love, he interprets it in childish terms.

The children of Kejser stores are character types who are assigned labels delineating one of their more prominent features. Eyvind Bauer has innocent, baby-blue eyes. He is the humble, fat clown whose humility so easily degenerates into hypocrisy. Feddersen is pike-eyed. He is the fishy-eyed terrorist devoid of human compassion. Avnsöe is a nervous bungler who prances about as if he had St. Vitus dance. Klara is referred to as a year-old kid. Martin Lind is constantly referred to as having a splintered mind. As labels suggest unidimensionality, the inhabitants of Kejser stores are reduced to unidimensional types incapable of growth and development.

Name symbolism, common to most of Branner's production, is another device which is used to typify characters. Ingolf Trane, tall and gangling like a crane, represents stiff formality and awkward decency. Skovman is an *Urmensch* and represents thoughtless animal sensuality. Martin Lind is the pliable young man who depends on the advice of others to direct his life. Herman Kejser sees himself as an imperious commander. Mrs. Ejerman is overly possessive, Miss Kirkegaard is as silent as a cemetery, and Golderman is a sterile banker.

In *Legetöj* we find character types which recur again and again in Branner's production.[57] There is the strong man whose power is only apparent and who seeks to dominate others. Feddersen is the prime example in *Legetöj*. There is also the strong man whose power is real enough, but who also represents the wrong use of power, as Ditmarc, who has no feeling for personal involvement or responsibility. There is the weak, ineffectual clown, as represented by Bauer, Avnsöe and Skovman. Herman Kejser is the pale, fat clown who retreats from a conflict at every turn. His constant refrain is: "Whatever you do is all right, but please keep me out of it." Finally, there is the transitional type who is weak at the outset, but who, as the result of a crisis and the galactic power of love and its consequent understanding, is transformed into a strong character with a sense of commitment, involvement, and social responsibility. Such is Martin Lind, the quintessential Branner protagonist, who ends by wanting to become a doctor to research the people in the gray zone between normal and abnormal.

There are also three basic types of woman; though here, too, there is a great deal of room for variation. There is the "good" woman, like Klara, a nascent version of Merete Rude in *Drömmen om en Kvinde*. She possesses an alogical lucidity and considerable charm, in consequence of which her doings, her sufferings, or whatever take on importance. She is practical, capable, and a delightfully refreshing creature, but she is seldom creative, cerebral, or overly complex. She can cut a clean swath through a man's overly-intellectualized despair and enable him to see an ultimate reality. This is what Klara accomplishes for Martin. Then there is the woman who is purely sensual. Although we do not actually meet her in *Legetöj*, Evelyn Avnsöe might be considered a nascent version of this type. Finally, there is the perverse, sterile woman who cannot fulfill her role as a responsible and responsive adult. Often, as is the case with Agnes Kejser and Evelyn Avnsöe, she turns to material objects as the center of her life, and both Agnes and Evelyn suffer from "furniture psychosis." [58]

In *Legetöj* Branner uses the device of presenting sequential reactions to the same event to afford glimpses of his "types." [59] For example, we follow Bauer and Kitty, Avnsöe and Evelyn, and Klara and Martin to the same film. That almost a third of the employees of Kejser stores saw the same film on the same evening stretches the reader's credibility to the limit, and the author intrudes to remedy this:

Beginnings through Legetöj

Millionaire for a Day had only received mediocre mention in the papers, but at any rate it played at four of the city's cinemas, and that evening alone it was seen by roughly three thousand people.[60]

One of the goals of the collective novel is to give an objective, impressionistic view of both the individual and the group. Objectivity is perhaps best accomplished when the narrator disappears as much as possible as a direct commentator and makes only oblique intrusions; i.e. disappears behind the mask of his characters, so that it is almost impossible to distinguish between the voice of the narrator and the voice of the character. It is such oblique intrusion that permits us to "feel" individually, to come face to face with a character, but to "understand" collectively without the direction of an ubiquitous narrator. A fine example of oblique intrusion in *Legetöj* is the scene in which Klara Kvistgaard visits Martin Lind for the first time:

"You're certainly a dangerous person," she says and looks at him fully for the first time. But surely he isn't dangerous. What he has experienced is so petty and ordinary—he smiles slightly—something lies in the background and shines through. Perhaps he is dangerous just the same; a lion alone with a kid.[61]

Or again in the scene between Klara and Martin in Dyrehaven:

She sat a little way from him with her legs drawn under her. The black dress with the many pleats was drawn tightly over her parted knees, and otherwise she sat quite still and chewed a little on a straw of grass. So far she had been driven by her sex that she sat here in the dusk at a slight distance from a man. He must surely go the rest of the way . . .[62]

The last sentence may or may not reflect the voice of the narrator. The pivot point in deciding between these two possibilities is, it seems to me, the word *surely*. Once it is deleted, we have the direct intrusion of the narrator. If it is retained, we have two possibilities: either the narrator is telling us that Martin must go the rest of the way, or Klara is telling us that she thinks that Martin must go the rest of the way.

Legetöj is a promising debut novel, but it is certainly not a great novel, and it ranks far below the best of Branner's production. It is interesting both as a period piece and as an introduction to Branner for the serious Branner reader. It incorporates many of the themes and plots found in his early short stories. Feddersen's plot to oust Ingolf Trane from Kejser stores is a reworking of *Isaksen*. Herman Skjold-Lassen in *To Minutters Stilhed* shares some features with Herman Kejser. The powerful influence of the medium of the cinema in *Bogholder Mortensen og Greta Garbo* comes through again in *Legetöj* when we see how Bauer and Avnsöe are influenced by *Millionaire for a Day*. Nevertheless, even in its genre, *Legetöj* hardly measures up to Hans Kirk's *Fiskerne*, indisputably one of the finest Danish collective novels of the time. Its techniques and patterns are well suited to conveying his ideological and thematic concerns, and this is perhaps the most doctrinaire of Branner's novels. By presenting Martin Lind as a young hero and expressing his will to become, that doctrine takes the form of a positive affirmation of personal freedom, one of Branner's major concerns. Branner was never again to embrace a consciously ideological superstructure. The thematic and effective patterns of his subsequent novels were to convey not so much a set of beliefs as a collage of attitudes. His insistence on the integrity of the individual and the humanitarian ethic of personal freedom was to continue, but that insistence was not to take the form of a moralistic enterprise so typical of ideological fiction. Instead, he was to explore intensely personal mental regions with his visual imagination and to express specific attitudes captured by that imagination, the most fundamental of which are his insistence on the freedom of independent maturation, the galactic forces of mutual love and understanding and the dilemma of freedom versus social responsibility.

CHAPTER 2

Barnet Leger ved Stranden, Drömmen om en Kvinde, *and* Historien om Börge

I Barnet leger ved Stranden

BRANNER'S second novel, *Barnet leger ved Stranden* (1937), is the story of Claus Böje's attempt to understand himself and grasp the truth about his unsuccessful marriage. As a means to these ends Claus writes a diary which forms the contents of the novel. Claus Böje's purpose in writing his diary is, as Jörn Vosmar succinctly says, to see whether or not it is "at all possible to establih a nexus between words and reality."[1] *Barnet leger ved Stranden* is as different in form and content from *Legetöj* as two novels can be. Nevertheless, in at least one important respect this novel may be seen as a continuation of *Legetöj*: Claus Böje is the same weak, pliable person as Martin Lind, and he conducts the search Martin Lind intended to make, for he probes his mind from the dark regions of abnormality through to the white regions of normality. One might even regard Claus Böje as an older Martin Lind married to a Klara Kvistgaard who has gone sour. Then, too, *Barnet leger ved Stranden* may be regarded as an expanded and revised version in novel form of the early play, *Eftermæle*. The argument of both of these works, as well as of *Legetöj*, is related to the general problem of idealism, i.e. the problem of defining the relation between the external world of experience and the nature of the self. The interest of Claus Böje and Martin Lind, as of all idealists, is in defining the true nature of this relation. The dichotomy between the two is manifested as an internal schism in Claus Böje's character: he cannot reconcile sexual choice with the idealism his father has inculcated.

Barnet leger ved Stranden is divided into four sections. In the first section Claus lays the historical groundwork as he describes the break-up of his marriage to Birgitte. He tells how he first met her as a classmate and how she even then represented female sensuality to him. She was a vigorous, sensual animal. To his father she represented the depravity of sex. Claus had begged Birgitte to marry him, but she had repeatedly refused. She then became a model for Hans Egge, a noted sculptor who had once carved a copulating couple. When Hans Egge no longer had any use for her, she then agreed to Claus's demand and married him. Shortly after they were married Torkild was born. Claus then became a victim of the Strindberg complex and began to suspect that Hans Egge was the father of the child. His marriage then deteriorated from bad to worse, until it was finally discovered that Birgitte had, in fact, been unfaithful to Claus. Claus immediately obtained a divorce. Afterward he returned to his boyhood home where he began to write the diary which comprises the first part of the novel.

The second part of the novel is the diary Claus wrote at a cottage to which he retired one spring in order to reflect on his past. Filled with loneliness and despair, he retreats within himself and plumbs the depths of his soul in an attempt to discover inner resources of character and absolve himself of the sense of guilt he begins to feel. At the outset he blamed Birgitte alone for the failure of their marriage, but he slowly begins to realize that he, too, may have been guilty for its failure. The haunting vision of the drowned Torkild appears before him as he sits alone in the cottage, and he begins to realize that his own actions, the way he treated Torkild, probably played a part in causing the child to commit suicide.[2] Having imagined that he has seen the specter of death in the form of a man with an axe, he locks himself inside the cottage and boards up the doors and windows. Finally his angst drives him to attempt suicide, and he tries to drown himself as Torkild has done, but the attempt ends in ludicrous failure.

In the third part of the novel Claus meets Doctor Torsteinson, the dipsomaniac who comes to treat the ankle he sprained in his suicide attempt. At first Claus views Torsteinson as a tactless intruder upon his self-imposed privacy. Torsteinson questions him about his past, why he has boarded up the cottage, and what has led him to such depths of depression. Through continued contact with Torsteinson, a sort of Doctor Relling figure, Claus begins to overcome his sense of anxiety, and the specter of beckoning death, the man with the axe, disappears:

But first there came an instant when I froze, as it were, on the threshold between consciousness and unconsciousness, and at that instant the man with the axe died—he became fused together with Torsteinson and vanished.[3]

At the close of the third part Claus meets Minna Halvorsen, another convalescent who has retreated from the world. Minna maintains that her psychiatrist has transformed her into a free and happy being. She claims to be liberated, emancipated from the restrictions of marital fidelity:

> I just see things more deeply and strongly than before. I'm free from anxiety and pangs of conscience. Completely happy and healthy.[4]

She asserts that Freudian psychiatric treatment cured her and enabled her to overcome her sense of anxiety. She, like Claus, is the victim of a puritanical childhood, and she claims that the miracle of modern psychology has freed her from the constraints of her past. Torsteinson immediately points out that anxiety is the life giving force. Once, he asserts, one is freed from angst, one is cut off from the primordial meaning of existence:

> You're free from anxiety, but if I were your doctor, I would give anxiety back to you, all of your anxiety. If only you could still have another attack of hysteria, if only you could scream and kick—but be happy.[5]

Though Torsteinson's words prove to be prophetic, Claus falls under Minna's spell and subscribes to her belief in the omnipotence of modern psychology. He simplistically reasons that if she has been cured by psychiatric help, then there may still be hope for him. He rejects what he calls Torsteinson's "horse cure," and he repeatedly visits Minna to learn more about her cure. She flirts with him and, although he denies that he is sexually attracted to her, he is finally driven to make a pass at her, and she flees screaming. They have discussed their childhoods. She has loaned him books on psychoanalysis and Freud. However, when she flees, he realizes that she has no more been liberated from her puritanical past than he has. Her flight breaks the spell of the psychological cure, and this is all too obviously indicated symbolically by a change in the weather. When she flees, the summer drought is broken, and it begins to rain.

In the fourth part of the novel Claus resumes his contact with Torsteinson. From September to January he practically moves in with Torsteinson and his wife Karen. In this final section, thanks to Torsteinson, Claus is relieved of his personal despair and gains emotional maturity. At the close of this section Claus Böje, the weak man who has doubted his masculinity and regarded himself as a fat clown, accompanies Torsteinson through a snowstorm to bring a new life into the world. That new life is Claus Böje's. In the storm he becomes separated from Torsteinson and reflects upon the relation between his experiences and his inner nature. Crouching in a potato pit in the swirling snow, he sees the apparition of the man with the axe once more. The vision of death and self-destruction has returned, but Claus musters his new-found strength and emerges from the storm to return to Torsteinson's house. The novel then concludes with a vision of hope on the horizon, a conclusion very similar to that in *Trommerne* and *Angst*:

At any rate, I can glimpse the top of the hill in a vague outline behind the white darkness, and when I get clear up I can see a light down in the grove on the other side. Dizzy a moment, I sense that it is a sign from heaven, a fire lit for me. But there's nothing supernatural about it, as I can see when I get a little further down the slope. It's only the illuminated window panes in Torsteinson's house.[6]

Finally, the myth that Freudian psychology is a panacea for emotional disturbance is conclusively exploded. Claus Böje has concluded his pilgrim's progress from the depths of despair to emotional maturity and self acceptance.

The four parts of the novel may be summarized as follows: Part One sketches the background of an emotional crisis; Part Two describes the depths of despair and personal anxiety; Part Three depicts the contact between a weak and a strong man and shows us Claus Böje on the road back to emotional health; and Part Four concludes when Claus finally achieves self acceptance on a quest with Torsteinson. When the four parts are summarized in this way, then certain similarities between this novel and Branner's masterpiece, *Ingen kender Natten* (1955), become clear. Claus

Böje is roughly equivalent to the self-doubting Tomas in *Ingen kender Natten*. Like Tomas, Claus must reach the depths of despair before he can hope to be cured. Like Claus, Tomas meets a strong man on a quest and is ultimately cured. However, Tomas, unlike Claus, must lose his life in order to gain it. Then, too, both novels conclude with a vision of hope.[7] Of course, the similarities are largely formal. It is the first person point of view which distinguishes *Barnet leger ved Stranden* from Branner's other long novels. In tone and theme it reminds one very much of Martin A. Hansen's *Lögneren* (1950), for both chronicle an author-narrator's attempt to overcome personal doubt and discover the true nature of the link between external reality and the inner self. Then, too, Claus Böje and the protagonist of *Lögneren* share the same need for masks and intellectual disguises.

Having outlined *Barnet leger ved Stranden* and designated its place within the canon of Branner's works, we now subject it to a more detailed analysis.

Branner's control of Claus Böje's narrative is extremely subtle and reveals his indebtedness to Hamsun. As Claus proceeds toward emotional stability, the narrative tone becomes less subjective and more objective. The subjective asides in the first two sections are largely lacking in the two final sections. At the outset Claus says that his purpose in writing the journal is to subjectively probe his individual *Sein an sich*:

In reality I felt a great sense of relief in telling the story in just this form. My pangs of conscience became less sharp. I halfway believed it myself.[8]

Claus Böje, like Glahn in Hamsun's *Pan*, is the solitary observer who attempts to establish contact with his past and with other human beings through retrospective reflection. He seeks to replace his subjective, angst-ridden view of the world with an objective view of reality. In his inner monologue he conducts a search for an absolute, objective answer to his problems. Toward the end of the first section his rambling definition of sorrow belies his divided nature and shows him incapable of thinking in terms of absolutes:

Sorrow can be a thousand things. It can be solemn and confident like the starry August night. It can be as desolate and hopeless as the eternal winter of the Arctic. It can have an unhealthy odor of decay about it. It can be frivolous and adorn itself with black tinsel, and it can be a means to hate people and dominate people. . . . Nothing is of any use without attempting to see things clearly as they are.[9]

Branner's debt to Hamsun is obvious in the imagery expressed in such passages—the book's poetic logic. As in many of the contemplative passages in *Pan*, the rhythm is uneven and disjunctive; sentences are humped together and the train of thought shuffles back and forth with the sensitivity of a seismograph. Claus's inner confusion is reflected in his spasmodic associations which, like Glahn's in *Pan*, vacillate between bitterness and affection as he attempts to relate to exponents of nature. This passage is a typifying instance of the spontaneous identification Hamsun and Branner constantly found between image and meaning, between the exponents of nature and what they symbolize. For both authors the conception of nature is significant by virtue of how man's intellectual character relates to it.

Claus Böje is imbued with the classical tragic flaw: in his attempt to see things clearly, he sees nothing and everything. Subjectively, he attempted to gain an objective view of truth and reality, and that attempt creates the inner tension of the first two sections of the novel. These sections, like Karin Michaelis's novel *Justine*, are the journal of an emotionally disturbed person who believes that his problems will be solved if he can define their causes. As soon as he reestablishes contact with society, Claus Böje realizes that simple, objective truths are essentially static and can only survive apart from the organic growth and development which human contact affords. Immediately after he meets Torsteinson, he formulates a new view:

. . . what purpose would it serve if I had tried to explain to him that simple truths are always lies and must necessarily be so; that truth is never clear and simple, but cloudy, complicated, and interminable.[10]

After he meets Dr. Torsteinson, Claus begins to take part in the give and take of life, and it is this realization of communicability which divides *Barnet leger ved Stranden* into two major sections. In the first two parts Claus withdraws from society, and in the third and fourth parts he becomes progressively more and more a part of the society about him until he resolves his problems.

Nevertheless, even before he meets Dr. Torsteinson, we note that he has made a significant step toward resolving his problems when, at the close of Part Two, he accepts his share of guilt:

> That's not the truth. That's a one-sided view, even that, but it's always a little less clear and mendacious. It's always a bit deeper. One can probe deeper still and ask if any responsibility is possible at all. But for me it's a moral and not a dialectical problem. I must accept my guilt and live or die with it.[11]

For Claus Böje self-criticism takes the form of self-seeking, which results in a discovery of identity and his growing awareness of the elusive reality of his individuality. He has said yes to the question of whether or not he can be answerable to himself for something concerning himself: he has accepted his guilt. In so doing he has taken the first step toward identity and in turn his emancipation from a restrictive dependence on the will of others in planning his life. Faced with the failure of his marriage, Claus was placed in a situation in which he had to make a choice: either 1) to attempt a rapprochement with Birgitte or 2) to carry out the divorce his family demanded. He had never been free to make a choice in his life. His job was chosen for him. The furniture in his and Birgitte's flat was chosen for him. In failing to make an independent choice, one fails, as Sartre has often pointed out, to become aware of one's subjective being. It was only when he was divorced and alone in the cottage that he became aware of his guilt, his subjective existence. The motifs of identity and self-discovery are just as haunting to Claus Böje as they are to Stendhal's Lucien Leuwen, who also composes the poetry of inadequate conjecture: What am I? What do I know about myself? Finally, in answer to his questions, Claus Böje says: "So what if Hans Egge really was the father of my child. I have no right to claim a title of ownership to the child's life." Claus Böje has begun to understand the necessity of relativism in judging the right context of reality; i.e. in determining the true relation between external experience and the nature of the self.[12]

Subjectively, Claus sees himself as a clown, and he repeatedly doubts his masculinity.[13] As his name implies (*böje*="to bend"), Claus is a weak, vacillating character. In direct contrast to Claus's weakness there is the sensual strength of Dr. Torsteinson and

Hans Egge. Hans Egge is the sculptor of the libido. Torsteinson is the robust sustainer of life. They are symbolically related through the medium of Egge's miniature of a nursing child which Torsteinson has on his desk. Claus Böje realizes Egge and Torsteinson as one and the same person. He begins by hating them both and ends by admiring them. Their figures have been blended together until they have become one:

> In a way Hans Egge has been my ideal: I hated him and admired him, because I ascribed to him precisely those qualities I myself lacked and coveted. The same is true of Torsteinson. In my fantasy Hans Egge and Torsteinson are actually one and the same person.[14]

Branner's use of name symbolism further unites Hans Egge and Torsteinson, as both have "strong" names, i.e. names which call forth visions of strong saga figures. Note, too, that Claus's son is called Torkild, another name with saga associations. Claus's reactions to both Egge and Torsteinson are overly sensitive and irrational, and, as Jörn Vosmar states, "these two men represent one side of the narrator's conflict," namely, his doubts about his masculinity. However, these doubts are but ancillary manifestations of one aspect of his conflict, the conflict between biological adulthood and spiritually debilitating dependency on the one hand and idealism and freedom on the other. It is a conflict in which the sterile idealism of Claus's father and the animalistic sensuality as represented by Birgitte, as well as Hans Egge and Torsteinson, are in an obvious rivalry for the domination of Claus's sensibility. Claus Böje is caught in the same conflict in which Paul Morel is trapped in D. H. Lawrence's *Sons and Lovers*: Paul Morel stands trapped between the unequivocal life force represented by his father and the sterile idealism of his mother. Then, too, Claus Böje reflects the same ambivalent attitude toward Egge and Torsteinson as Paul Morel does toward his father—an attitude which pendulates between hate for his sensual crudity and admiration for his simple masculine integrity. His inability to integrate these attitudes with the actualities of experience turns Claus inward on himself to seek the shape of reality, and this quest results in the self-inventory that is his diary. Thus, technically (the spontaneous identification between image and meaning) and thematically,

Branner's *Barnet leger ved Stranden* appears to stand in close relation to D. H. Lawrence's *Sons and Lovers*.

Torsteinson is finally reduced to normal proportions in Claus's eyes when it is revealed that he is a dipsomaniac. After the revelation of this weakness, Claus and Torsteinson are united on their quest through the snow storm. They have never addressed each other in the familar before, but during their struggle through the snow, Torsteinson suddenly addresses Claus as *du,* a verbal expression of the equanimity and ties that now reign between them. In the snow storm Claus learns that it is the struggle to sustain life which itself returns life-sustaining force. It is this realization which marks the final stage in the process of his individuation and signifies that Claus has resolved his conflict.

Just prior to the emergence of a vision of hope at the conclusion of the novel, Claus hears the cry of a newborn child, and that cry resounds within him:

> But somewhere in a distant house a newborn child screams, a child asserts its obstinate life in the midst of the freezing space. I hear the child crying deep within myself, and I feel it as millions of ice floes drift far out in the black storm.[15]

Claus Böje has come to accept the demands which Branner sets forth in a later short story, *Et grædende Barn,* and he is cured the moment he realizes and accepts these demands:

> There must come a moment when the adult accepts himself with all his inevitable defects and takes his responsibility upon himself.[16]

As Mogens Bröndsted has shown, the title of this novel stems from a poem in Björnson's *Arne*:[17]

> Oh, Lord, take in your hand
> The child who plays by the strand . . .

and Bröndsted suggests that

> . . . the title's associations shall not be interpreted as signifying some free condition of innocence; it designates human weakness (in contrast to God's might), and its original occurrence points toward

consciousness of guilt and maternal need, toward the desire to obtain forgiveness and peace in the soul. That is precisely the protagonist's, Claus Böje's, situation.[18]

The first occurrence of the image of the child playing by the shore in Branner's works is in the short story *Bogholder Mortensen og Greta Garbo* (1934):

Mortensen, the bookkeeper, played hazardously like a child on the shore, played farther away from house and home and marriage.

From the contents of this story it is clear that Mortensen is playing a game in order to escape from reality into the realm of fantasy, the very game Claus Böje attempts to play. However, in *Barnet leger ved Stranden* the title has at least two important associations. Although it may denote Claus Böje's attempted escape, it was also by the shore that Torkild made his final escape from the miseries of his childhood. Given Bröndsted's interpretation of the title's associations and its quality of a *Leitmotiv* designating a flight from reality, we note that it expresses a fundamental concept in Branner's writings: human weakness, defined as the inability to accept one's responsibilities and one's self, often results in a tragic flight from reality. Claus Böje's flight results in a maddening vision of death, but through the agency of Torsteinson he is brought face to face with reality and accepts it, and the vision of death vanishes. As the protagonist in a drama of the vulnerability of the idealist, Claus Böje shares spiritual kinship with Ibsen's Johannes Rosmer in *Rosmersholm* (1886): both represent the dilemma between the will to progress and accept life and the conservative inheritance.[19] Claus's attempted suicide further relates him to Rosmer's leap into the millrace. We have already noted that Torsteinson plays a role similar to that of Relling in *The Wild Duck* (1884). Then, too, Torsteinson shares many features with Ulrik Brendel in *Rosmersholm*: both allow their visions to be drowned in drink when acutely aware of their poverty of ideals and its consequent spiritual paralysis. As Brendel for Rosmer, Torsteinson represents a nightmare version of Claus's own dilemma. It is the recognition of this relationship which draws Claus to Torsteinson during their symbolic quest through the storm. Torsteinson seems capable of making the same statement as Ulrik Brendel makes about Peter Mortensgaard that Mortensgaard "is capable of living his life without ideals. And that, do you see—that is the mighty secret of action and victory. It is the sum of the whole world's wisdom." A further relationship with Ibsen's tragedies of idealism is Birgitte's characterization as a sort of Nora figure who also breaks with an idealistic husband. It is not altogether surprising that *Barnet leger ved Stranden* has many ties to Ibsen's naturalistic chamber plays, his tragedies of idealism, such as *A Doll's House, The Wild Duck,* and *Rosmersholm,* when we recall that this novel is obviously an expanded and revised version of Branner's naturalistic chamber play, *Eftermæle* (1933), in which Ibsen's influence is all too obvious. However, Branner's imaginative technique, self-conscious psychologizing and restatement of Claus's dilemma in terms that remind us of D. H. Lawrence remove *Barnet leger ved Stranden* from the Ibsenesque drawing room and relate it to Scandinavian literature of the 1930s. Claus's flight finds its closest parallel in contemporaneous Scandinavian literature in Aksel Sandemose's *En flyktning krysser sitt spor* (1933), and in tone it is strongly reminiscent of Sigurd Hoel's *Fjorten dager för frostnettene* (1935), whose Dr. Holmen is possessed of the same angst-ridden vision as Claus Böje. Then, too, Birgitte, as seen through Claus's eyes, can be compared to Vibeke in Helge Krog's *Oppbrud* (1936). Vibeke, like Nora and Birgitte, also breaks from her husband to form a new and independent life. Like *Barnet leger ved Stranden, Oppbrud* seems all too packed with thoughts and spiritual retorts which sometimes bankrupt its narrative power and convert it into a set piece.

Barnet leger ved Stranden is the only one of Branner's novels which was not, at his request, republished. As he says in *Glimt af mig selv,* he considered it a failure.[20] One may object to much that we find in the novel, but we may never know exactly what Branner himself held to be its most objectionable faults. Jörn Vosmar asserts that "the symbolism is a bit too massive to be in harmony with the intimate form of the diary,"[21] and he supports this assertion with a series of examples. However, the symbolism in this novel is neither more nor less massive than that which we find in Branner's more successful novels, such as *Rytteren* and *Ingen kender Natten.* Vosmar also asserts that the novel's first part is its best.[22] Nevertheless, it can be objected that the self-analysis of this section is overextended and repetitive. Then, too, if the purpose of the diary point of view is to convey a sense of immediacy and let us follow the course of Claus's emotional development directly, then the tone of distance in this section is out of place with the overall formal restrictions of the diary style in the following sections.[23] In contrast to Vosmar, Frederiksen concludes that *Barnet leger ved Stranden* is a particularly talented novel, carefully composed and treats one of the grandest of literary themes: that life becomes death.[24] Frederiksen also asserts that:

It presents occasions for psychoanalytic studies. It talks about a person's different views of art all the while he passes through his various phases. It discusses the double directions of guilt: toward a decline into the cultivation of defeat and in the opposite direction toward a heavy-handed will to life.[25]

Nevertheless, Branner's excessive use of Freudian psychology and its attendant emphasis on sexual symbolism detract from the novel's artistic qualities. In form the novel is an all too programmatic, banal, and almost clinical study of a person who probes his psychic depths, uncovers the roots of his problems, gains insight, and is finally cured through renewed contact with his fellow men. Branner comes perilously close to using psychoanalysis for its own sake and not as an interpretive tool to provide an expanded vision of the inner workings of the mind. From a letter written while he was still at work on the novel we can infer that Branner was well aware of these problems and that the novel might fail for these very reasons:

Naturally, social incongruities are to blame for this, but in my opinion the problem also has a psychological side, and that's what I want to take up—also in a forthcoming novel which will treat problems of upbringing. There are enough authors who treat the economic structure of society, and though it's indeed true that such is needed, I've seen my problem as finding a new consistency in psychology. Don't forget that this too is a social problem. Previous authors have treated psychological matters for art's own sake, and I don't know of any more disgusting task. Although Freud may have been mistaken in many things, he's still the one who's given psychology a fruitful and constructive impulse. I don't believe a bit in his dream theories and his "sexualization" of the whole of the subconscious, but he's nevertheless shown that such things exist and play a role in man's thoughts and actions . . . . In my next book I'll presumably abandon the collective novel's form and concentrate on a single person, but not to present a picturesque ruin for contemplation, but, if possible, to arrive at some basic laws. In all probability it won't succeed, but it may put another author on the right track who will carry it to a conclusion.[26]

This is probably one of the most revealing statements Branner ever recorded concerning his attitude toward Freudian psychology. From this letter, as well as from some passages in *Barnet leger ved Stranden,* we can infer that Branner may have been aware of the debate between Dr. Sigurd Næsgaard and the critic, Kai Friis Möller, as well as Paul la Cour's comments on Freudianism in literature. In order to gain a better understanding of the impact Freudianism made on Danish literature during the 1930s we would do well to review this controversy in some detail. First we note that, though there are many elements of Freudian psychology in *Legetöj,* they play a subordinate role and character development is not, as in *Barnet leger ved Stranden,* presented in the form of psychological diagnosis. The Freudian concepts of fixation and regression are, of course, quite obvious in *Legetöj.* For example, there is Herman Kejser's narcissistic Napoleon fixation and Martin Lind's mother fixation in his relations with Klara Kvistgaard. As is shown in the letter quoted above, one of the major tasks Branner had set for himself in writing *Barnet leger ved Stranden* was to find new relationships in psychology. It is also clear that he did not agree with Freudian psychology completely, but regarded it as one of several interpretive tools and was well aware of the danger inherent in placing too much emphasis on Freudian interpretations alone.

In an article in 1932 Paul la Cour stated his disapproval of the overwhelming emphasis contemporary Danish literature was placing on psychoanalysis, and Branner *may* have been familiar with la Cour's article. The article, "Freud og litteraturen," [27] is so important to our understanding of the contemporaneous feeling toward psychoanalysis in literature that it deserves to be quoted at length. In this article—in which he also expresses his reactions to Karin Michaelis's *Justine,* Aksel Sandemose's *En sjömann går i land* and Karo Espeseth's *Sår som ennu blör,* la Cour states that:

> What they find in psychoanalysis—and indeed it's incontestable that, almost without exception, those poets who are influenced by it know it only at third or fourth hand—is a pathological template to work

from, since they don't even take the trouble to vary, by personal effort of ingenuity, the cases which are presented.[28]

While the first condition for a literature which wants to avail itself of the means which psychoanalysis can actually afford the poet should be to employ the method only for the elucidation of psychological phenomena which are still unknown, at the moment most literature sinks to the level of the easiest of all—the ready-made and commentated pathological picture.[29]

Wherever mysticism and romanticism enter into the novel, there's a prompt dissolution of its esthetic structure. When one no longer operates with psychology, but with a pathological picture that's firmly moulded once and for all by science, then paraphrasing in a very summary and undifferentiated manner cannot be avoided. The delicate calm and continuity which the psychological novel demands to gradually and as exhaustively as possible elucidate a person's mind can hardly harmonize with the strong, pathological effect one intends when one embraces the psychoanalytic pathological picture. Style is necessarily driven to bustling nervousness, driven from its epic lair to a lyrical one.[30]

With some modifications the critical remarks above apply to *Barnet leger ved Stranden.* We have already noted that the novel's tightly knit structure may be broken down and summarized as steps in a case history of mental illness. Given la Cour's criticism of this approach, Branner's appraisal of Freudian psychology and the statement that he felt that *Barnet leger ved Stranden* was an artistic failure, we may conclude that Branner believed the novel to be too much a psychological case history and not enough a piece of art. Simplistically, Branner probably felt that he had not succeeded in subordinating the terms of the psychological approach to character analysis and presentation to the larger themes of guilt and responsibility in a description of the process of individuation. In short, he may have felt that he had merely presented a case history and not taken the trouble, as la Cour points out, to vary the case which he presented.

A year after the appearance of Paul la Cour's article, Kai Friis Möller wrote a scathing review in *Ekstrabladet*[31] of Dr. Sigurd Næsgaard's popular handbook, *Psykoanalyse*,[32] and entered into a debate with Dr. Næsgaard. Dr. Næsgaard, a well-known popularizer of Freud, was probably encouraged in his efforts by Professor August Wimmer's successful experiments in psychology. He was totally in favor of the sexualization of the subconscious which Branner rejects in his letter.

One is tempted to infer that Dr. Næsgaard was the actual counterpart of Minna Halvorsen's psychiatrist in *Barnet leger ved Stranden*:

"The clever fellow's probably your psychiatrist. What's his name?"
She said his name.
"Has he analyzed you?"
"Analyzed!"—Mrs. Halvorsen cringed slightly at the word—"We've talked together."
"About your childhood?"
"Among other things, yes."
"While you lay on a sofa, and he sat behind a screen?"
Mrs. Halvorsen laughed aloud. "It isn't done that way anymore. One talks together as one person to another."
"Have you then had your inhibitions broken down? Have you discovered what crimes your parents committed against you while you lay in the cradle?" [33]

. . .
"The usual doctor's pride, eh: we others understand nothing."
"No, because you can't see things in their proper perspective. And you're personally involved, and one never understands a thing when one is personally involved. The foremost cancer researcher we've ever had died of cancer without suspecting it. He died with the belief that it was a benign disease. Take him as an example. Hold off with such talk about inhibitions and complexes. That's children's play with matches. Life is formed of inhibitions and complexes. Life consists of contrasts. You go around with an internal tumor which sucks strength and color from things and makes symbols of them. It sucks out a little Freud. It bounds life within imaginary forms to overcome it more easily. Every day it grows a little bit as cancer tissue grows on normal tissue. One can already begin to smell it." [34]

Having outlined the controversy which arose after the impact of Freudianism became apparent in the Danish literature of the 1930s, it appears that these passages may reflect the controversy, as well as Branner's own view of psychology. If so, then Branner saw Freudian psychology as a doctrine against which he reacted on at least two points: it offers oversimplified, and therefore deceptive, absolute explanations; and, as it is rooted in determinism, it absolves one of personal guilt and responsibility. In view of Branner's comments in his letter to Holger Kristiansen, it is obvious that he believed that psychoanalysis had some heuristic value, for it revealed a portion of the truth. We note that Claus Böje begins his quest by searching for absolute truths, the absolute truths which Freudian psychology as a general theory seems to provide. He probes back into his childhood and upbringing and finds a partial answer to his present reactions. During his childhood his father had frequently punished him by locking him in a dark closet.[35] Gradually he realizes that that repression was the beginning of his destiny. In revenge he had punished Torkild in similar ways. Unreasoned punishment had driven Torkild to suicide, and that was the ultimate cause of the breakup of his marriage. Torkild was victimized by his father in much the same way that many characters in Sigurd Hoel's *Möte ved milepelen* (1947) were victimized by their fathers. Hoel's characters commit some petty mistake as children, and they are severely punished. They do not understand why what they did was wrong, nor do they understand why they were punished. The result is an abiding sense of guilt throughout adult life. Though Claus found the source of his guilt in an infantile repression, he was not absolved of his sense of guilt. On the contrary, he began to feel more keenly. In practice the Freudian "absolute" cure is, Branner is saying, powerless to absolve personal guilt or to induce one to take on the responsibilities inherent in accepting it. Thus, although *Barnet leger ved Stranden* suffers acutely from an over-indulgence in psychologizing, it clearly represents the interplay of weakness, guilt and responsibility, concepts which were to occupy key positions in all of Branner's subsequent discussions of the human situation.

II Drömmen om en Kvinde

Four years after *Barnet leger ved Stranden,* Branner published his third novel, *Drömmen om en Kvinde* (1941).[36] Upon publication *Drömmen om en Kvinde* received mixed reviews. The story takes place on the eve of World War II. At the opening of the book we meet Knud Mortimer, a lawyer who has come to Copenhagen to be operated for cancer, and his wife, Charlotte. Both are seated at a card table where they are playing bridge with their hostess, Merete Rude, who is awaiting the birth of her first child, and Mimi Fleischer, one of Mortimer's former clients. Beyond the

Barnet leger ved Stranden

bridge game, all Europe is waiting tensely for the outbreak of the war. Knud Mortimer is waiting for Merete's husband, Niels, to return home. He hopes to be able to discuss his tragic condition with him. After Niels returns home, Knud Mortimer suffers an acute attack of intestinal pain. Charlotte then drives him back to their hotel. Shortly thereafter, Merete feels the onset of labor pains, and Niels calls a car to take them to the hospital. In the second part of the novel Mortimer dies in his hotel room, the war breaks out, and Merete gives birth to a son. Warned by the doctor that Merete might have a difficult delivery, Niels has been terribly worried about Merete and believes that his son's birth is nothing less than a miracle. He stands dazed by the miracle of birth as he hears that the war has broken out.

To say that *Drömmen om en Kvinde* contains rich symbolism, illustrates a masterful use of the stream-of-consciousness technique, provides superb examples of characterization by antithesis, and affords an almost unlimited variety of interpretations would, while true, only be a way of listing some of the novel's formal aspects. Perhaps the best way of approaching the novel is to discuss it thematically. Earlier, we concluded that one of the central themes of *Legetöj* was the contrast between an idealized version of reality and reality as it actually presents itself, and one of the major themes of *Barnet leger ved Stranden* is the necessity for ethical relativism in judging the right context of reality. I suggest that one of the major themes in *Drömmen om en Kvinde* is the necessity for resignation to and reconciliation with reality, reality in personal relationships as well as in all its aspects. This interpretation appears to be in line with comments Branner made in an interview shortly after the novel was published:

> . . . and then I also wanted to portray people's flagging capacity to confront the greatest things, life and death. It is a matter of people's dishonesty with themselves and others. . . . Each time a person boasts, even a child can see through the boast, but all of us do it just the same. People are naive. They see through others, but they don't see that others use the same tricks as they.[37]

Furthermore, by contrasting the dying Mortimer with Merete who is to give birth, *Drömmen om en Kvinde* relates the two major origins of experience, birth and death, and implies that emotional maturity is only possible if we resign ourselves to and accept these realities.

In *Drömmen om en Kvinde* interpersonal relations are presented in terms of antithetical characterizations. One character is antithetically played off against another with contrapuntal skill. Consider, for example, the antithesis between Merete Rude and Mimi Fleischer. Mimi's character is entirely centered around her relations to material objects and her inability to establish contact with human beings, while Merete delights in human contact and she has a devil-may-care attitude toward material things. Knud Mortimer is a coldly calculating rationalist, while Niels Rude is completely negative. The positive qualities we find in one character are completely lacking in that character's counterpart. The plus and minus shuffle of these antithetically contrasted characters is centered around their varied reactions to life and death. They are kaleidoscopically shuffled as they react to these two essential experiences of existence.

Their reactions are revealed in the form of intrapersonal monologues which convey the impression of a stream of consciousness. Past and present events intermingle in a character's consciousness, and things happen by random association rather than by any scheme of causation. The monologues of various characters are spliced together with little or no narrative connective, so that it is sometimes difficult to tell when the reflections of one character stop and the reflections of another begin. The overall effect of spliced inner monologues is that of a collective consciousness; the collective reflections of all of society are recorded simultaneously. As past and present mingle together, it is impossible to maintain a fixed concept of time and the logical sequence of events. Consider, for example, the inner monologue in which Mortimer rationalizes his resignation to and reconciliation with the reality of death and thereby realizes his conception of God. He weighs and considers and evaluates the disparate facets of his experiences and synthesizes them into a unified realization of what his death will mean to his life:

Death, he thought and failed to notice that he was being helped down onto the stretcher and lifted up, for me death shall be the only thing which is greater than humanity. There are many other things

Barnet leger ved Stranden

which are greater than mankind, but I didn't experience them. I've met them a thousand times in my life. I've always had them with me, but I didn't know it. I only needed to have looked out of my window. I only needed to have bent over. I only needed to have summoned them, so that they would have come, but finally I'm meeting that which is larger than humanity, for no thought or word can make death into something humane. For me death shall first become God.[38]

Here, in one of the most important passages in the novel, Mortimer generates the evaluation he has set on the meaning of experience, the experience of having lived and lost. Mortimer is a fragmented man, splintered into facets which only fit together into a unified whole when he attempts to summarize his spiritual thinking on thinking in the face of death. Intellect, emotion and perception are at war, and Mortimer's vision of life has been one of massive personal disintegration. Branner's triumph as a novelist is to have turned that disintegration into a firm backbone of the literary form of *Drömmen om en Kvinde*. Mortimer's stream of consciousness unravels like a thread from a bouncing ball which always returns to the same spot. And this is reflected stylistically by a new thought: I only needed to + A, I only needed to + B, . . . etc.

The two major origins of experience, birth and death, are contrasted within the context of a psychotherapeutic experience. The novel presents a stage full of characters where, in Heidegger's phrase, the dreadful has already happened. People have gone off the path of life: they have lost sight of the meaning of the fundamental experiences of life: mature love (Charlotte, Merete, Niels, Mortimer), death (Mortimer), human relations (Mimi, Charlotte, Eva, Björndal) and personal integrity (Björndal, Charlotte). They then undergo a psychotherapeutic experience: a search for something lost validated by the experience of experience.

The opening scene of this psychotherapeutic experience is a bridge game. Around the bridge table we see a foursome of antitheses: Knud Mortimer, a head without genitals; Charlotte, who is the reverse of this; Mimi Fleischer, the sterile woman who is only capable of contracting relationships with things; and Merete Rude, the archetypal "good" woman.

For Mortimer the bridge game represents the game of life; it takes on the same symbolic significance as the medieval chess game. For him the game and its logical superstructure are far more important than the identities of his partners. His life has been bounded by his concern for absolutes, for arid, abstract concepts, and throughout his life he has embraced secularism: a closed attitude toward life that shuts out all possibility of transcendence and dogmatically declares that this world is all there is. He has closed his eyes to the reality of the mystical experience. In contrast to Mortimer, Merete Rude is thoroughly non-secular and alogical. She is the archetypal "good" woman associated with birth, warmth, protection, fertility, growth, and abundance. This is symbolized by her dress, which is a loose fitting sack-like garment the color of rich, brown earth. She wants to cut through the overly intellectualized ideals in man's world with the non-cerebral, archetypal values she represents. In this she is an expanded version of Klara Kvistgaard, and she is clearly aware of her non-secular approach to life:

Whenever he was gone she hopped over into his bed in order to lie doubled up in the snug depression left by his body to sense him with her skin. She laughed at him in the dark, laughed and called him every possible tender and meaningless and desperate name—oh, let him come home and let me tweak his ears and pull his hair. Let me jerk him and bump him. I'm laughing. Can you hear that I'm laughing at you?— Yes, it's you I'm laughing at. I'm laughing at your dreams and stars. I'm laughing at your symbols and systems. I'm laughing at your temples and your gods. I'm laughing at you with your taboos and your self-torment and your solemn silence. . . . But he wouldn't understand it if she laughed at him and said those sorts of meaningless things. It was so desperate that he understood nothing about her, absolutely nothing about a woman.[39]

Merete's mystical approach to life is contrasted with Mortimer's attempts to interpret mysticism logically. The contrast is shown in a set of parallel scenes in which first Mortimer and then Merete enter a Gothic cathedral. They are not, strictly speaking, reflecting on the meaning of Christianity, but on their relationship with, and reaction to, the spiritual element in life.[40] Mortimer has located the cathedral (= spiritual values) on a map, and he reads the guidebook's statement that the irregularities of its architecture "gave it the look of irresistible organic growth; the human spirit's

Barnet leger ved Stranden

slow growth toward God."[41] Mortimer fails to see the organic growth, man's gradual reconciliation with spiritual values. He views the Gothic ornaments only as ornaments. Seeing the nuns gathering offerings, he reflects on the mercenary side of organized religion. Slowly, however, he is caught up in the rationale of the irrational:

> He was also slightly cold. Just upon coming in he had felt the gray stony cold as something beneficent, but now he was chilled by it. The room was metamorphosed before his very eyes. It was no longer bright and streaked with sunlight, but gloomy and oppressive. And it didn't help him any that the organ began to play at that very moment. It was like a resounding tone of darkness up under the vaults, a darkness of dead centuries. He laid his neck back and could almost see it undulating up there. He became ill and faint from it. His eyes rapidly had to find something to concentrate on. They found a window toward the west, a high ogive window where the virgin sat with the child on her lap. Her robe stood out immensely large and blue against the late sun behind the interior, and while he looked up at it, it was as if everything became bathed in dark blue tones, and the sun in the west was like a dark blue blotch. He became faint and wanted to take hold of something, a person, an arm. But his hands found nothing to grasp, and he noticed how he began to sink.[42]

Thus Mortimer reaches out for human contact at the very moment he begins to lose contact with the forces of rationality which have left him devoid of feeling. That Mortimer attempts to make contact with his hands is pregnant with symbolic meaning.

The significance of hands as emblematic of a person's character is discernible throughout *Drömmen om en Kvinde*. Charlotte has "loose" hands, and she is a loose woman. Eva, Mimi Fleischer's impotent confidante, has helpless hands. The dying Mortimer has a shadowy hand. Merete has swollen, brown hands, and she repeatedly[43] looks forward to the time when her child will discover its hands; i.e. begin to discover itself as a human being. Charlotte has the habit of stroking the back of Mortimer's hand with her thumb whenever she is struggling to gain some sort of affection from him. She does so immediately after Mortimer's cathedral scene, and Mortimer then tells her to leave him,[44] for he still cannot grasp the human contact he is seeking. Merete takes Mortimer's hand after he has collapsed at the bridge table. She places his hand in her lap, and Mortimer reveals his affection for her.[45]

The cathedral scene with Merete begins in direct contrast to that with Mortimer. She finds the cathedral haphazardly. She is distracted from contemplating its architectural joys, for she is occupied with watching the children who are playing outside it. She feeds the pigeons in the square and watches the children's reactions to her feeding the pigeons. She is absorbed by the joys of life, and the cathedral makes her aware of her insignificance, of her mortality:

And at the same time she felt how she would be obliterated and perish in a brief moment. She noted how it became darker and darker far below where she sat. But she would continue to look upward. Her eyes sought something which they could concentrate on, and at last they located a great shining window toward the west.[46]

The results of the two cathedral scenes are the same: a feeling of anxiety is generated in the eye of the observer. For Mortimer it is angst for having come into contact with life when on the brink of death, and for Merete it is angst for having to lose her life when giving birth to life. Nevertheless, their sense of angst is not the neurotic sort Claus Böje feels in *Barnet leger ved Stranden*, but the condition of dread, the anxiety of the existentialist. In his survey of Branner's works, Sven Möller Kristensen comments as follows on the introduction of existential elements into Branner's writings:

From a psychoanalytic point of departure, Branner turns more and more in the course of time to a contemporary view of the entire human situation and of the fundamental problems of life, life and death, whereby his works come into contact with postwar existentialism. It is already noticeable in the novel, *Drömmen om en Kvinde*. . . .[47]

The existentialist elements in *Drömmen om en Kvinde* are perhaps most noticeable in the parallel cathedral scenes. Existentialists hold that contemplation of the irrational leads to despair, which, as an end in itself, is a desirable state of mind. Despair is seen as a necessary and desirable achievement, for only by it is man able to appreciate fully the nature of existence. All those incapable of despair, of angst, are cut off from facing and being aware of the meaning of reality. The individual confronts reality in his own way and in isolation, as when Mortimer and Merete are

Barnet leger ved Stranden

alone in the cathedral. When the individual faces reality intensely, the world as it is objectively given ceases to exist, and he turns inward upon his own contemplation of the irrationality of existence: the cathedral *qua* cathedral ceases to have a purely objective existence for Mortimer and Merete as they turn inward upon their own contemplations and their eyes are drawn toward the window in the west. When, existentialists maintain, we are faced with the reality of death, an essentially irrational event, our existence becomes "essential" and meaningful, because death anxiety becomes a basic state of our minds. We must then learn to accept this state of anxiety as a fundamental condition of our existence. In the cathedral Mortimer and Merete learn to accept the necessity of being resigned to and reconciled with this fundamental condition.

In contrast to Mortimer and Merete who reflect on the significance of their observations, there is Niels Rude who can only observe. When he returns home from work, he pauses before his house and peers through a window. He sees the bridge players as fish in an aquarium illuminated by a green light. Mortimer, Charlotte, and Mimi are reflected in the green light as sterile, cold fish. They are robots devoid of human feelings, and, as in *Legetöj*, the fish image delineates automaton characters incapable of making contact with life. Mimi's mouth is decribed as quivering like a fish's, and the thick skin around her mouth is white like a fish's skin.[48] When Niels views the bridge players through the window, the fish image is taken up again.[49] It is played upon for a while,[50] and then dropped until Niels stares into Charlotte's fish-like face after Mortimer has collapsed at the bridge table.[51] It is then taken up again when Charlotte imagines that the bar in which she and her lover, Björndal, are sitting is a large aquarium.[52] Mortimer, like Feddersen in *Legetöj*, is a pike. While Charlotte, Mimi and Mortimer all appear to Niels as if they were submerged in the green light of an aquarium, Merete stands apart in a brown light outside the opaque, green light of the aquarium.[53] The fish people in *Drömmen om en Kvinde,* as is indicated by the use of the same image in the short story *Om lidt er vi borte,* are trapped. A glass screen of illusions separates them from a reconciliation with the spiritual elements of life and from life itself.

As in *Legetöj*, we find a plethora of child similes in *Drömmen om en Kvinde*.[54] Mimi is childish, and Merete has the face of a child. Clemens, Merete's doctor, whom we are to meet later in *Rytteren,* has a child's eyes. Merete and Niels play at love like children, and Charlotte places Mortimer in bed and undresses him as if he were a child. While Merete and Niels are on their way to the hospital, they sit holding hands like children. When Mortimer is suffering the agony of the death throes, Charlotte treats him as if he were a child. When Merete is to deliver her child, Niels sits with her and they hold hands like children. When Mimi Fleischer believes that Charlotte and Eva are plotting to take her possessions away, she reacts like a recalcitrant child and threatens to burn everything she owns. Thus, as in *Legetöj* and *Barnet leger ved Stranden,* whenever adults are confronted with a crisis they undergo an infantile regression, for they can only accept reality with a child's fanciful vision.

Though Mortimer and Merete reflect upon death with a mature sense of despair, Niels views death with the eyes of a child. Reflecting upon his childhood, Merete views Niels as follows:

. . . he sat silently in thought over the dead rabbit and tried to understand why it was so quiet and completely stiff. He knew full well that it was what is called "dead," but he didn't want to understand what that was.[55]

In the face of death Niels, like Börge in *Et Barn og en Mus,* clings to a death myth.

Merete realizes Niels as a dreamer and a child, a child and an assailant, who has never grown out of his childish views, never undergone the process of maturation and individuation:

. . . he was still like a child who bleeds and doesn't want to realize that the red is blood. He remained standing with a dead animal between his hands and didn't want to understand that the animal was dead. Ever since early childhood he would come to her and demand that she return his dead animals to life.[56]

To Niels, Merete represents a fairy-tale princess who has the magic power to transform death into life. She is the prepubescent dream of a woman who, like Maria Magdalene in *Ingen kender Natten,* is to transform him by sexually giving rebirth to him after the iterative death of intercourse:

Barnet leger ved Stranden

He demanded that she be his death, as bitter and salty as his death. He wanted to drown and perish within her. But when he awakened after death, she was to be the green and solid earth he rested on. He came to her as a stranger from dark centuries in which the bloody and barbaric bonfire and stake and offertory pyre flamed. He came with his sex's burden of anxiety and hate and demanded she be his offertory lamb. And when it was all over, when he had dreamt and struggled and hated and feared, he wanted to double himself up and hide beside her, and she should be a cavity of darkness about him and the warm mother's milk in his mouth.[57]

Perhaps the reader will be struck by how this passage, as well as much else in *Drömmen om en Kvinde,* is strongly reminiscent of Hemingway, particularly in *For Whom the Bell Tolls* (1940), and I am thinking specifically of the well known passage in that novel in which Robert Jordan makes love to Maria.[58]

Branner was admittedly influenced by Hemingway.[59] Having been introduced to Scandinavian authors in Gyldendal's *Gule serie* under the editorship of Sigurd Hoel, Hemingway exerted an enormous influence on contemporary Scandinavian literature. Both authors employed a highly developed sensitivity to convey the relationship between the diversity of nature and the human experience, and in both novels there is a conscious awareness of the breakdown of institutional humanism—the conflict of logic and the alogical, the conflict between science and the church. In both novels the central theme is an affirmation of life which, while passionate enough, is moving only in itself, while the contrast with death only serves to heighten that affirmation. However, it is in matters of style that the relationship between the two is clearest: in both novels we find the same simple rhythms, the succession of coordinate clauses which suggests a disparate view. Then, too, there is the same lack of mental arrangement, for things are seen and felt disjunctively, one after the other and without reflective synthesis.

Merete is the dream of the warm and protective mother Niels lost when a child and, as such, she represents the same thing to him as Klara Kvistgaard represents to Martin Lind. Their lovemaking is the innocent game of children who mingle together and lose their separate identities:

Are we children playing that we're adults, or are we already adults playing that we're children? We smile to each other and begin a totally new game. We notice something like footsteps which approach from afar, footsteps, footsteps deep in the blood, and we know that it's a game of life and death. We smile and hold each other captive with our eyes. We approach each other on a swaying silver thread spanning the dark. We meet in the middle and dance and swing each other around. We let go and leave each other. We run forth and meet again. We swirl about each other, closer and closer. We play and leap like two dolphins over the deep, a light and a dark dolphin.[60]

The voice of a child cries out within Niels and Merete, just as it cries out within Claus Böje at the conclusion of *Barnet leger ved Stranden:*

I hear the child crying deep within myself, and I feel it as millions of ice floes drift far out into the black storm.[61]

In one of the most lyrical passages in the novel Merete hears the voice of a crying child. She falls asleep in a chair after she has withdrawn from the bridge game while waiting for Niels to return home. She dreams that she has wandered into a strange, enchanted forest, where she hears a child crying, and she tries desperately to locate it:

In the pine forest it had sounded like the barbarous game of children in the quiet afternoon. A child's trumpet and drum behind the trunks. A short while ago it had been an old man's mumbling and grumbling monologue. But now when she paused and listened intently it sounded like an infant which was crying helplessly somewhere in the distance. It seemed to her that she must find that child. She must console it and quiet its crying. She hastened her pace and walked toward the sound, and it continued to be just as far away, and every time she stood still and listened, it came from another direction. At the same time it seemed as if the crying became weaker and, being completely frightened, she thought that the child might die if she didn't find it soon. She began to run, now in one direction, now in another. At last she came to a dark and enclosed grove where nothing stood erect and nothing was green—fungus encrusted and crippled trees bent like serpents toward the ground. . . . The child had disappeared in this grove, for she heard its cry stronger now, but she didn't know in which direction she should search. She came deeper and deeper into the fugitive tangle of roots and branches. Finally, she could neither go forward nor backward, and she had to sit down a while to get her breath.[62]

Barnet leger ved Stranden

In her search to discover the child crying within her Merete could, as Emil Frederiksen suggests,[63] very well have composed the following poem about her imaginary adventure in the forest:

> I hear a child crying somewhere,
> Back many a dark mile,
> And it is I who shall find that child
> And I'll make it once again smile.
>
> I wonder where it's crying, in you? in me?
> Perhaps on a foreign star,
> Perhaps in a gray old man
> In a little village afar.
>
> I don't know, I only hear it,
> The still cry flowing.
> —And should it stop, the child's dead
> And I am unknowing.[64]

This, the only poem Branner ever published, crystallizes the mood and metaphor of his theme of the child in the adult. Once, he is saying, the child's cry is stifled in the adult, then the adult, the full-grown child, shall die. There must remain in each of us the insatiable fire the child has for experience. Once we have reduced life to a sterile, logical system and can no longer, as Torsteinson can, experience it as something mysterious, then we have killed the child within us and we are doomed to spiritual death. The child similes in *Drömmen om en Kvinde* do not, therefore, have the ironic tone they have in *Legetöj*, for here they are used to express a poignant sense of sorrow for those who have stifled the cry of the child within them.

In an important scene prior to Merete's dream of the child crying in the forest, Mortimer reflects on his imminent death. Mortimer, who was called the radical in his youth and who reduced everything to an arid, logical system, now cries out helplessly. He cries out like a helpless child, and it may be his cry that Merete hears:

A flame bursts forth in one's loins, and in an instant it's crumpled together—puff, gone. It's never had any validity. One has conceived of it in abstracts, and now it applies to me—me! Every other human being shall live. I am the only one who shall die. One stretches out one's hand to something one knows, something one's familiar with, but there isn't anything at all. They've all passed away together in a great, silent earthquake. How does it help me that my thoughts have believed in a principle, a law, a reality beyond human comprehension, when my guts scream in fear of a living God? [65]

After Mortimer has cried out and Merete has heard the child's cry in the forest, she awakens and goes to say good-bye to him. She holds his hand tenderly and calls him "uncle" and sits down beside him. They are to meet but once again when they are spiritually united in the parallel cathedral scenes and become reconciled to death.

Whenever people are faced with a crisis of indecision in *Drömmen om en Kvinde,* they suddenly feel as if they cannot rise to act. For example, Charlotte feels that she cannot get up from the bridge table, and she later feels that she cannot get up from the table when she is seated in the bar with her lover, Björndal. The motive of physical immobility at a time of crisis is repeated again in *Ingen kender Natten* when Tomas cannot rise from his chair to act. This is but another example of Branner's use of one of a basic set of motives in varied contexts. This kaleidoscopic reshuffling of the same basic motives is a major aspect of his imaginative technique and further indicates that his art seeks to construct a collage of attitudes, rather than a set of beliefs.

Finally, as we have seen, much of *Drömmen om en Kvinde* is cast in the form of dreamlike, semiconscious inner monologues. This is not altogether a new device for Branner, for, as we noted previously, he used it very effectively in *Legetöj* when Martin Lind revealed himself to himself in an inner monologue. In *Drömmen om en Kvinde,* however, the inner monologues are not merely brief snatches but extended over many pages and usually cast in the form of dreams, such as Merete's dream of the enchanted forest. Though Branner undoubtedly learned much from both Virginia Woolf and James Joyce in the use of this device, he has made an important innovation by dramatizing consciousness in dreamlike sequences which are spliced together with little or no narrative connective. It is also to his credit that he does not fall prey to the self-conscious psychologizing in the inner monologues in *Drömmen om en Kvinde* which we find to excess in *Barnet leger ved Stranden.* Though we find psychological insights, they are not couched in Freudian jargon. Many of these monologues relate the dreams of Jungian *animæ,* man's archetypal image of the opposite sex which he carries in his personal and collective consciousness.[66] They are revealed by various characters as dreamlike projections of the women in their lives. Charlotte is Björndal's dream of a wonderfully sinful woman. Merete is Niel's dream of the warm and protective mother he lost as a child. Merete is also Knud Mortimer's dream of the daughter he never permitted himself to have.

By showing us the process of resignation to and reconciliation with life and death vis-à-vis the dream of a woman Branner reveals the process of individuation: he shows us how the individual must consciously and subconsciously learn to resign himself to and reconcile himself with the various aspects, favorable and unfavorable, of his total self. Mortimer and Merete suffer from death neurosis until they learn to recognize, confront, and accept the vital necessity of death anxiety. In the cathedral they learn to accept the rationale of the irrational: to accept death in life by reinterpreting it as life in death. Branner depicts the same theme in the short story *Shagpiben.* The story's central figure began by saying no to death and ended with a victorious yes after having resigned herself to its reality.

As in his previous novels, Branner uses name symbolism in *Drömmen om en Kvinde* to label his characters and thereby expose one of their essential traits: Mortimer < Lat. *mortuus,* Clemens < Lat. *clementia.* Niels Rude (*rude,* "pane of glass") is a transparent observer. Carl Björndal (*björn,* "bear") represents animalistic sensuality.

In *Drömmen om en Kvinde* Branner had moved from the attempt to symbolically express the currents of sensation between characters, as in *Barnet leger ved Stranden* and in Lawrence, to the effort to reflect the ideas, feelings, and impressions in individual minds, as in Joyce and Virginia Woolf. For him technique became, not an objective in itself, but a discovery procedure, and the discovery was the neo-orthodox view that reason (Mortimer) can prove only that the nonexistence of God is absurd, while the positive assertion, that God exists, can only come by means of revelation. It is in his statement of this view, presented within the context of impending death and birth, that he espouses elements of postwar existentialism in what may in time prove one of his finest novels.

III Historien om Börge

If *Drömmen om en Kvinde* is a semi-mythical tale of individuation, then *Historien om Börge* (1942) [67] is certainly a continuation of the same tale, except here the chronology is turned back to childhood. *Historien om Börge*, originally given as a series of twelve radio readings, is formally related to Branner's short stories, and each of the twelve sections can almost be read as a self-contained unit. The thread which connects them is the story of a young boy during four years (at ages 4 and 5, and 8 and 9) of his life. It is difficult to fit *Historien* into the developmental chain of Branner's other works, and it occupies relatively the same position with respect to his other works as, say, *Hemsöborna* does with respect to Strindberg's other works. It lacks the symbolic devices, the inner monologues, the chains of similes, and many of the character types, such as the archetypal "good" woman, present in so many of Branner's works. Nevertheless, *Historien* treats many of the same themes found in his three previous novels. Strangely enough, it has usually been passed over very briefly by serious Branner critics, such as Jörn Vosmar and Emil Frederiksen. Vosmar dismisses it in four pages.[68] This seems strange when one learns that Branner himself regarded the first six sections as some of the finest writing he ever did,[69] and this novel may be one of the finer descriptions of childhood produced by a Scandinavian author.

Börge, whom we met earlier in *Et Barn og en Mus*, begins his life in splendid isolation. His world is bounded by his parents, Gokke, the maid, and the fence surrounding his yard. The garden is a fantastic paradise, an innocent Garden of Eden populated with an imaginary menagerie of tigers, whales, and elephants. Börge is a lonely, sheltered child who is the sole master of his imaginary world and who has an extraordinary power for fantasy. His flights of fantasy lead him to believe that reality is fantasy and vice versa. For example, he realizes the God he has been told about as a thoroughly homomorphic being:

> God was the very carpenter who called. His voice was high up above the trees, and he was very angry.[70]
> God was angry. He waited to hear God's voice come out of the high, high board fence where the world ended.[71]

Barnet leger ved Stranden

Börge's relations with his father do not have the same immediacy as those with his mother. His father has been sick, has been abroad, and he has seldom been allowed to approach his father directly. For Börge, then, his father has the character of "otherness," of remoteness and externality. These are precisely the same qualities that the adults in his environment have ascribed to God, so it is only natural that he identify his father with God:

> And his father was still greater. He stood in the middle of the world and built the ship. His father was *God* and built the ship.[72]

Börge sees his father as his protector and believes him to be infinitely wise and strong, giving the comfort of security. Branner is suggesting that nothing is so relevant to the child's development of the concept of God as his early relations with his father. This is an idea which occurs again in both *Rytteren* and *Söskende*.

The seclusion of Börge's world is shattered when Eva (= Eve) enters his Garden of Eden, his private world of fantasy. Eva is stronger than Börge, more worldly wise, more perceptive, and has a greater sense of self-assertion. She destroys his world of fantasy by ridiculing it:

> The garden of paradise with all the animals who came when he called. It was just as if it didn't exist any more.[73]

Eva also fantasizes for him, but it is with a conscious purpose that she does so. She wants to control him by making him doubt the reality of his fantasies. She wants to dominate him to overcome her own sense of insecurity which is the result of her having been raised in a broken home. Her sense of insecurity becomes obvious when, having alienated Börge, she tries to regain his confidence:

> He didn't cry. He didn't do that anymore. He just walked a little way off and wouldn't play. But then she came flying up to him and grabbed him around the neck and placed her cheek to his. Little Börge, I didn't mean it, little Börge.[74]

Börge is unaware of her insecurity and, therefore, incapable of using it to achieve a balanced relationship with her. He simply has no understanding, intuitive or acquired, of the psychological composition of those about him. He is an unreflective observer, a younger version of Niels Rude. He merely senses, but cannot relate patterns of behavior in any meaningful way and has an animalistic reaction to life, like one of his imaginary animals. This reaction is conveyed by a stylistic device, a device often employed by the Norwegian novelist, Tarjei Vesaas. Börge is acutely aware of odors.[75]

There are certainly autobiographical traces in Branner's portrayal of Börge. In *Glimt af mig selv* Branner tells how he met woman for the first time when he was four years old. She was the girl next door who alternately amused him and terrorized him:

And she knew what hell was, for all her family were Catholics. She told me about purgatory and the devil. "And you'll end up down there, because you're not Catholic," she said. Then I cried. But she grabbed me around the neck and dried my eyes with her hair and said that I should be married to her and become Catholic. She would certainly see that I didn't go to hell.[76]

A further instance of Eva's attempts to control Börge is when she ridicules his mother for merely being another foolish adult.[77] She is attempting to wean him away from her mother and into her power. Finally Börge wishes that she had never destroyed his world of fantasy, for he senses a loss of innocence brought about by his relations with her. Nevertheless, the damage has already been done, and he longs for her to come and play with him, as he no longer feels self-sufficient in his world of illusions. She has made him question the sense of security he once felt, for she has supplanted his former illusions with a new illusion, i.e. adults are fools:

But he didn't go up and say it. Long after she had left he sat in the hole next to the street with his knees drawn up under his chin. He wished she wasn't there. He wished she had never been in the garden with him. He wished the garden were the garden of paradise once more without her. But just the same he sat the whole time and kept his eyes on her gate.[78]

Börge's fantasies have obtained mythical projections: his father as God, his private menagerie, Eva as his mother and superior.

The effect of these projections is, as Jung would maintain, to isolate Börge from his environment. He no longer has a real relation with his environment, but only an illusory one. The more projections interpose themselves between Börge and his environment, the harder it becomes for him to see through his illusions. Then, as Börge begins to question the validity of his fantasies, he begins to confuse reality with fantasy: he becomes unable to distinguish between reality (= truth) and fantasy (= lies). The inability to make the distinction between the two causes Börge to lie and say that he has not heard his mother when she was calling him:

"No,"—that is the terrible thing that is called *to lie*. But he couldn't say anything else. For even if he had heard them, just the same he couldn't answer. And in a way he hadn't heard them either. He had been far away from them. He had been in a place where they were not. . . .[79]

Here Börge fails to make a clear distinction between reality and illusion and right and wrong. He has become so isolated from his environment that right and wrong and the subsequent punishment which wrongdoing carries with it no longer make it morally imperative for him not to lie. Truth simply does not exist in an illusory world. Nevertheless, to lie is, of course, wrong, and wrongdoing is followed by punishment. Eva makes this clear to Börge when she tells him that he will be arrested for writing on walls:

Yes, they can. Because when you've done something your father can't say anything. And even if the police haven't seen it, they know very well that it's you. They also know where you live. They know everything. And you'll land in prison. And from that prison you'll come into a room full of people, and there you'll be spanked with a big whip, while everyone sits and sees it.[80]

Later, he is told the same thing by his aunt when he has lied about having stolen a piece of chocolate. An obedience to rules is justified solely by an appeal to consequences, but the necessity for moral rules and obedience to them is never explained. Duty is never translated into purpose and the value of moral virtues. Failure to do so results in a failure to instill a pattern of reasoned ethical behavior in the child. Whenever a moral imperative is not justified in explanatory terms, it tends to become illusory. Thus Börge's first "crimes" are punished by the illusions of drastic consequences, the punishment of an all-seeing, all-knowing police force. Börge, in precisely the same way as Charlotte in *Drömmen om en Kvinde,* justifies his lies by a subconscious appeal to fantasy. As he cannot sort out a "real," wrong lie from a "real," right fabrication of fantasy, he is not certain when he has actually committed a crime and when he has not committed a crime. Therefore, he can easily be tormented by feeling guilty for unconscious conflicts not attachable to any conscious act. This explains why he feels guilty when he has not actually committed a theft at school. He feels guilty for a crime of fantasy and that fantastic punishers see his guilt. Here Branner shows us the consequences of not distinguishing between conflicting realities: the reality of fantasy vs. the fantasy of reality. He is also showing us how the individual begins to recognize himself as a person and becomes responsible for his actions.

One of the major themes in *Drömmen om en Kvinde* was the meaning of death for life. Branner takes up this theme again in *Historien om Börge.* In his infantile fantasy Börge plays at being dead.[81] When playing dead, to die is to close one's eyes and shut out the world. When his father dies, Börge visualizes death as a temporary departure and does not immediately realize the effects which death can have on adults:

. . . His father was dead now. He understood that clearly. But his father hadn't been there long, and he wasn't dead like birds and animals are dead, and not like other people either. His father would come back again. He knew that then. He didn't think so much about it. He thought more about the candles. He couldn't understand why his mother didn't want them.[82]

It is because Börge's father has died off stage, so to speak, that Börge makes a distinction between his father's death and the death of an animal, and he believes that he has only disappeared temporarily to return later.[83] Soon, however, Börge begins to realize how death affects others. He demands love and affection from his mother; but, because of her husband's death, she has withdrawn into a private world, said no to life, and cannot return the love Börge demands. In Freudian terms, identification with the death instinct has mastered Börge's mother's life instinct:

And if he said something to her, she didn't hear it. And if he shouted and she finally heard it, she would become very angry, though he hadn't done anything. He didn't understand it. He knew very well that she was that way because his father was dead, but he didn't understand it just the same.[84]

She tries to overcome the death instinct, but she simply cannot transcend her feelings. When his love for her is not reciprocated, then Börge begins to realize her as a playmate and to identify her with Eva. When he discovers that his mother cannot even partially take part in his world of fantasy, he then rejects the identification with Eva. Finally, he becomes frustrated and wishes to make his mother angry and thereby force her into some sort of emotional response. He fails even in this, and she remains unreceptive and unapproachable:

All the time she hopped around. She dropped down in thought with the light dress gathered about her knees. Just like Eva. But she didn't resemble Eva. She resembled a big strange bird. There was something vague and awkward about all the things she did. And now she was singing: "Patty cake, patty cake, on the morrow we'll bake." Just as if she weren't playing with him at all, but only with herself. Or with a little child . . . He couldn't bear it. Suddenly he picked up his pail and flung it into the water.

His mother got up slowly, and her eyes became big. She drew a deep breath and reached up to her hair. "Why did you do that, Börge?"

"I don't know." He didn't know either, he just did it. Perhaps it was to see if she would get mad. She stood a while. The trowel fell down into the sand. "Now you can play by yourself," she said and left him. . . .[85]

After his mother's attempted suicide by drowning, Borge is placed in the care of his paternal uncle. Confronted with the cold austerity of his uncle and aunt's sterile bourgeois home and his aunt's security neurosis (locking doors), sexual frustration and sublimation (scrubbing floors), the fabrications of fantasy begin to evaporate. A realistic view of death supplants his former fantastic view:

He knew that his father was dead. He wouldn't come back again. He was what's called dead. *Dead,* that's what he was.[86]

Börge feels insecure in his new environment. Affection is doled out in bitter-sweet drops. There is one respite: his uncle plays the fool to amuse Börge, and he becomes Börge's friend and takes him into his confidence. However, the possibility of Uncle Jörgen's becoming a substitute father figure is destroyed when Börge hears him crying:

> Sometimes she continued long after they had come up to the bedroom, and one night his uncle cried in there. Suddenly he lay awake and heard it. It was dreadful. He'd never heard a grown man cry before. He hardly believed it could happen.[87]

The destruction of Börge's uncle forms the basis of his character identification. By character identification I mean the conscious and unconscious acquisition of theoretical and practical knowledge whereby an individual projects himself into other people and adopts the character of people outside himself. By means of character identification we identify the roles people play in their relations with others and with ourselves. Having experienced his uncle's destruction, Börge learns to realize his subordinate role to his aunt and how his uncle will relate to his own problems. When he flees from his uncle and aunt, he reflects as follows:

> He must run again if he thought about her. She must not see him as the thief. But his uncle? Yes, he would believe it, but his aunt wouldn't believe it, and then his uncle couldn't help him.[88]

Börge is now capable of character identification and judgment. Earlier, it was impossible for him to realize that Eva was attempting to subordinate him to her will. Nevertheless, to demand that, having reached the level of development where he is capable of making character judgments, he also realizes why Eva wished to dominate him would be to demand too much maturity in a child.

It is extremely significant that Branner inserts the passage quoted above into the section entitled, *Flugten*. Börge's flight from his uncle and aunt is a cathartic experience. By fleeing from their essentially alien world, Börge effectively discharges the underlying pathology of his guilt fantasies. He frees himself from himself and takes the first steps on the path toward becoming an independent being. The amorphous plasticity of the infantile period has ended, and Börge has gained insight into the world about him. The period of character identification as one of uncritical absorption has ended, for Börge has developed the corrective power of reflective judgment to assess the value of each new person learned by identification. He has developed independent judgment and thereby become an independent being.

After his flight, Börge returns home to his mother and the garden, but his imaginary bestiary has evaporated in a mist of self-awareness. He develops a private life apart from his mother, and the bond of dependency between them is broken as he goes his own way:

"Come and take my hand," she said when the forest path began. "No," he shouted, "I'm playing something." But on the way home she held his hand, and he didn't take his hoop along anymore. He didn't want to go up there anymore at all. He wanted to play at home in the meantime, and he might very well do that too. She went alone. But he didn't play. He paced about in the garden and was annoyed. He wondered whether she would act differently toward him when she came home. At last he ran to meet her. No, she wasn't any different. But he didn't stay home anymore. Not before that day when he ran down to the swamp where *the boy* sat.[89]

At the close of the book Börge states his final attitude toward death:

"Yes, but I'm afraid of it just the same," he said. "I'm afraid to die. I don't understand why you have to die. Why don't you live forever." [90]

Whereas his mother now sees death as a servant of life, Börge views it as an enemy of life. It is because she has come to believe in life that she can accept death. For Börge, however, life is too new, too unfulfilled to relinquish. If Börge never experiences fulfillment, then he may end where Knud Mortimer begins in *Drömmen om en Kvinde*.

Historien om Börge takes us back to the origins of experience in what Northrop Frye would call a fable of identity and, as such, readily lends itself to the archetypal critical approach. It is framed in one of the great birth myths of all time, the myth of the Garden of Eden. Börge begins life in the fantastic garden of delight where he is innocent and secure and his father is God. The Garden of

Eden existence is, of course, not the ideal of life. It is the fantasy, the illusion of life. The fruits of knowledge enter the garden in the form of Eva. She destroys the garden as illusion. Börge is then driven from the garden and condemned to a life of suffering (reality principle) with his aunt and uncle. There he acquires the knowledge of good and evil, of character identification and judgment, and learns to distinguish between reality and fantasy. He flees from the reality principle and undergoes a cathartic experience in flight. Finally, unlike Adam and Eve, he returns to the garden, though the garden has been destroyed as a fantasy. The innocence of childhood has disappeared, and Börge emerges as an independent being well on the way to maturity.

We conclude that the four novels, *Legetöj*, *Barnet leger ved Stranden*, *Drömmen om en Kvinde*, and *Historien om Börge*, are widely divergent in format, if not in theme. In all four the protagonists are confronted with crises of consciousness and search within themselves to discover depths of character which will enable them to overcome their crises. Martin Lind decides to abandon the sterile world of business to research the gray region between normality and abnormality. Claus Böje conducts a personal research of that region, the region in which he feels himself located. Knud Mortimer and Merete Rude confront death with despair and learn to accept their personal angst as a fundamental life-giving force. The portrait of Börge is a portrait of a small boy who develops the emotional tools that will forge him into an independent being capable of overcoming crises of consciousness.

Varied in form and structure as they are, all four of these novels represent experiments in the development of a distinctive style and form. *Legetöj*, essentially a collective novel, is an example of one of the most popular genres of the era in which it was written. Its excessive use of character labels, similes, and all too programmatic introductions vitiates its artistic qualities, but it remains a promising debut. *Barnet leger ved Stranden* is a failure, for Branner had not yet learned to use psychology as an interpretive device, rather than the sole vector of characterization. *Drömmen om en Kvinde* breaks the restrictive bonds of the psychological novel and, with its skillful use of the stream-of-consciousness technique, it is a major step forward for Branner as a creative writer. If one were to select one of these three novels as representative of the mature Branner, then *Drömmen om en Kvinde* would probably receive the nomination. As it treats the themes of death, life and anxiety which are so important to the whole of Branner's subsequent authorship, it not only represents a major concentration of insights into the world Branner projects, but it also gives a penetrating analysis of themes germane to any novel which broaches higher seriousness. *Historien om Börge* is a charming, penetrating and valid portrayal of a child's early life with universal appeal. As such, it is certainly the most successful of Branner's first four novels and probably has staying power, though it seems to lack that immediacy of characterization which induces a feeling of empathy in the reader. Thus, with the publication of his first four novels, Branner was still in a formative stage, groping for the form and style necessary to convey his highly personal interpretation of the world about him.

CHAPTER 3

The Art of the Short Story

EARLIER we reviewed Branner's short-story production through 1936, the year in which *Legetöj* appeared. Until that time all of his short stories had appeared in the Sunday supplements of various Danish newspapers. These supplements were a regular feature of the Danish press and included personal interest stories, discussions of art and literature, and a short story or two. Three years after *Legetöj* nine of Branner's previously published stories (*Isaksen, Et Barn og en Mus, Sjukos Sjæl, Hannibals Træsko, Lördag Aften, Iris, Kameliadamen, De blaa Undulater,* and *Pengemagt*) together with the previously unpublished story, *Om lidt er vi borte,* were published as a collection with the title, *Om lidt er vi borte*.[1]

As a writer of short stories, Branner represented an anomaly among his contemporaries, for the short story had almost disappeared from the Danish literary scene during the 1930s, until the various Sunday supplements, such as *Politiken's Magasinet, Social-Demokraten's Hjemmets Söndag* and *Nationaltidende's Söndag,* had given it a new impetus by providing a new outlet. It was here that Branner had made his start as a published author of short stories, but some of the best prose writers of the period—Knud Sönderby, Hans Kirk, Mogens Klitgaard, and Hans Scherfig, refrained from cultivating the short story. Hans Hertel has suggested that the Danish neglect of the short story was in part caused by the fact that: ". . . the simplifications and caricatures in the descriptions of people we meet in novels shine through more crudely in the shorter form." [2] Be that as it may, a practical reason for the neglect of the short story may have been economic. Publishers believed that a collection of short stories or an anthology simply would not sell as well as a novel and therefore did not encourage authors to write short stories. Consequently, short stories were regarded as a sort of literary stepchild. Elias Bredsdorff makes this point quite clear in an article in *Politiken* (June 18, 1941) in which he shows that short stories certainly had a market value in both the United States and Britain. He also suggests that the average Danish reader probably preferred to buy short stories in the form of the Sunday supplements, rather than in book form, and he concludes with a challenge to Danish publishers to publish an anthology of the best Anglo-American short stories. A year later his anthology *18 Moderne Amerikanske Noveller* (1942) appeared. This anthology, containing stories by Erskine Caldwell, William Saroyan, Ernest Hemingway, and John Steinbeck, enjoyed an enormous success, and the door was forthwith opened for the publication of collections and anthologies of short stories by Danish authors. In the same year, the Copenhagen publishing firm of Carit Andersen brought out *30 danske noveller,* which contained H. C. Branner's *En halv Alen Vand.*[3] Two years later came Branner's second collection of short stories, *To Minutters Stilhed,*[4] which enjoyed the same success as his first collection.

From this brief recapitulation of a section of literary history we can see that Branner achieved his first successes with a genre which was shunned both by his contemporaries and by the publishing industry, and this fact is also brought out in Frederik Schyberg's review of *Om lidt er vi borte*:

> H. C. Branner made his debut with *Legetöj* and established his name. The weaker *Barnet leger ved Stranden* made a break in his reputation. Now his third book has come out and it is not a novel, but a collection of ten short stories. Short stories are not a great commodity, but these should become so. We have no finer talent in Danish prose than that which H. C. Branner demonstrates here.[5]

Perhaps it was, as Schyberg suggests in the same review, Branner's extraordinary ability to place the small world revealed in his short stories in a wider perspective that permitted his stories such an outstanding success:

> But Branner delivers his very best—as happens in *Lördag Aften* and *Om lidt er vi borte,* when he can bring the description of his small world into larger perspective, turn it into, so to speak, the center of a world picture, a focal point, apparently casually, but upon closer inspection of the deepest significance for life as it forms for all and in all. In some unforgettable episodes in *Midt i en jazztid* and *To men-*

nesker mödtes Knud Sönderby has operated with the same technique, but Branner has elaborated on this technique and cultivated it for use in those short episodes in which he really condenses his talent.[6]

It now remains for us to discuss the four remaining short stories in *Om lidt er vi borte*, as well as those in *To Minutters Stilhed* and a selection of other stories published elsewhere through 1949.

Kameliadamen[7] describes the wretched lives of a director of a provincial theater company and the members of his traveling company. The director is a homosexual in love with Willy Speth, who follows the company from one town to another. The young apprentice who plays Gustave is readily recognizable as the young Branner who played the same role, and he is laughed off the stage in the second act, as was Branner. Other than a display of a certain mastery of style and language, this story has little to offer except for the biographical light it casts on Branner.

De blaa Undulater[8] is perhaps one of the best stories in the collection and possibly one of Branner's finest technical achievements in the genre. Told in a crisp, rapid style, this story from childhood relates how nine-year-old Katrine trades the parakeets her father has given her for a top. Katrine has been hardened by life in a broken home. Ironically, it is not coldness, cruelty or lack of emotional warmth that has hardened her, but her father's mild-mannered behavior and lack of decisive emotional concern. Having heard that she has misbehaved at school, he tries to reason with her and mildly threatens to take her parakeets away from her. Her father genuinely wants to understand her and only wishes to treat her kindly, but she wants him to reprimand her violently, to break down her domineering attitude:

"I don't know," said Katrine. She would gladly have said something else, but she really didn't know what. She sat there tense, like a strange animal in a strange forest. She wished that he would shout out, beat her and scold her, somewhat hard and decisive. But she knew that he wouldn't do that, she knew it was coming now. He was already standing before her large and weak. She could notice the odor from his clothes.[9]

Katrine's neighbor and playmate, Nils, is, as we are told in the opening lines of the story, afraid of Katrine. Just as Börge in *Historien om Börge* is simultaneously attracted and frightened by

Eva, so Nils is attracted to Katrine and frightened by her cold-hearted attitude. In contrast to Katrine, Nils has been made meek and pliable by his father's austerity and is a product of the very disciplinary severity which Katrine demands. Katrine is a nascent version of Branner's cold, sterile woman figure, the Mimi Fleischer type. Nils, like Iris in *Iris,* is the weak person terrorized by a cold and domineering counterpart. Once Katrine's father has told her that she really loves her parakeets, then she immediately wants to get rid of them, for she feels tricked by her father and wishes to spite him. She gives them to Nils, and then one evening she comes to Nils's house to stare at them. He kindly offers to give them back to her, and she answers with a violent outburst:

"Shut up," she said. "Beat it. Beat it, you little mama's boy, you little kissy boy. Beat it back to your darling mother and grab her around the neck and kiss her for me."[10]

Nils's offer to return the parakeets has had the same effect on Katrine as has her father's assertion that she actually loved them. She has been so frozen by her father's mild, detached display of emotional concern that she inwardly demands a violent display of decisive action, elemental concern. Had Nils told her that the parakeets were his and his alone, then she would have respected him. Instead, she can only cry out and mock him for possessing the very things she intensely desires. Ineffectual emotional response is accompanied by alienation from the objects of love and emotional concern. This is the larger lesson of the story and the focal point of its narrative tension. Katrine's bitter response brings it out like the lash of a whip. The underlying cause of Katrine's condition is, of course, her father's myopic character judgment: one's misconceptions of another person's inward demands lead to loss of psychic contact and love. This loss and its causal order are the overriding concerns at the heart of Branner's best short stories.

In *Pengemagt*[11] unemployment threatens to dissolve a family. Relieved of his job, a man goes out in search of work. His pride is severely offended when, having been stared at like a marketable piece of meat, he is told that there is no opening for him. He returns home, feigns illness, and retires to bed. He then loses self-respect in the eyes of his wife and, thereby, his own self-confidence. Unable to earn money and assert himself, he reacts with a bitter outburst to his wife and son. Finally, however, he becomes reconciled with his wife, but they are no longer the same loving couple they once were. Now they are merely companions.

The final title story in *Om lidt er vi borte*[12] spells out the thematic unity for many of the stories in the collection. A man has wandered about alone for several days, has peeked through windows, silently observed those about him, and has finally returned to his wife to whom he attempts to explain why he has remained away. His observations are related in the third, rather than the first person, which permits the reader to view his observations obliquely and gives the story a wider perspective. Past, present, and future are blended together to give an impression of timelessness and diminish the span of a lifetime: in a little while we shall be gone, and this theme song is reenforced by the observer's words: "and in the morning he will sail." His impressions are placed in the perspective of the era in which he makes his observations, for he overhears and reflects upon conversations about the probability of the outbreak of the war. The storm clouds of World War II are gathering, and by reference to that event the story presents an individual and collective view of those clouds. The storm is symbolically suggested by the stormy weather through which the observer wanders. The storm's rush and noise tumble about in the wanderer's mind like the roar of distant cannons. The outer, physical atmosphere of a storm is reflected in the inner, disjunctive observations of the observer. After his return home, the wanderer attempts to explain himself, an attempt to summarize his personal *Weltanschauung* which, as it reflects some of the basic attitudes which occur and recur in Branner's writing, deserves to be quoted in full:

". . . one can walk around on the roads and peek in the windows at people and see how they can place a great deal of seriousness on things that are not serious at all. That's what's crazy about most people: they don't know that so few things are serious. Death is serious, but we hasten to find a name and a place for it and go over it with a rake and a spoon. But with you it's serious. I know that it's only an instant I have my arms around you. I can hear your blood calling to mine that in a little while we'll be gone, and my own blood answers back that we'll be gone in a little while. That joy won't always exist to be borne. Sometimes I must go my own way apart from it and feel unhappy and drag other people down into my unhappiness. I must make myself tiny like a child in the dark in order to understand it once more and bear it once more. But it's my joy that it's serious and not my unhappiness. The only thing that really matters is that we are still young and may still live an instant.[13]

Having heard his explanation for his absence, his wife puts her arms around him and says: "Hold tightly to me," she said, "oh, hold me tightly." [14] This is a recurrent replique throughout Branner's works; an expression of the necessity for mutual contact and understanding. Despite the exigencies of war and petty crises of the everyday sort, few things have a higher seriousness in life than death and mutual love, and love is a shield against the awareness of death. Only through an acceptance of death and the agency of mutual love can anxiety be overcome. Sometimes, however, anxiety in the face of death and the mutability of life get to be too much for the spirit to bear, and one must retreat from life and hide away like a small child. This is also the theme of a well-known poem, *Angst*, by the doctor poet Emil Aarestrup (1800–1856), the poem from which Branner probably took the theme of his story, as is shown by its second stanza:

> In a little while we'll be separated
> Like berries on the hedge.
> In a little while we'll have disappeared
> Like bubbles in a brook.[15]

Unlike *Om lidt er vi borte*, the majority of stories in *To Minutters Stilhed* are from childhood. In this second collection of stories the individual is once again seen in a wider perspective as his petty losses and victories are placed under the author's magnifying glass.

Skibet[16] is the first person narrative of an adult reflecting on an experience he had when eleven years old. The boy's ineffectual and dreamy father built him a model boat, and, as for Börge in *Historien om Börge*, the boat building established a bond of friendship between father and son. Johannes's brother Svend has Johannes show him the boat and then makes fun of it. He finally dares Johannes to drop it on the floor:

Then the ship fell. I don't know if I actually threw it, or if it just slipped from me; but I struggled desperately to save it in flight.[17]

The ship is shattered and Johannes fears the awful punishment he will receive when his father returns home. However, when his father does finally return home, Johannes sits beside him and cries and begs for mercy and forgiveness, but his father does not punish him. Instead, he says that Johannes should forgive him and he presents him with a flag. Like Katrine in *De blaa Undulater,* Johannes desperately wants to be punished by a strong, assertive father. His father's lack of a strong emotional response to his actions liquidates the sense of respect instilled by the boat building.

The Norwegian author Johan Borgen regards this story as not only central to Branner's authorship, but as forming a point of departure for the impulses which later recur in his more complicated works. Johan Borgen has given a fine interpretation of this story which is perhaps equally appropriate for *De blaa Undulater:*

> Rash critics would conclude from this situation that H. C. Branner means that it would have been better if the father had been firm. But I don't believe this was the presentation intended by our poet. It's something else. Once again in yet another impressive and quiet course of action he establishes that the weak person longs for punishment, for force, that he is willing to submit himself to tyranny—rather than move in an atmosphere of mildness and understanding which places such a terrifyingly heavy burden of responsibility on a person.[18]

The theme of the weak person's desire for violent emotional response in the face of his inability to accept the responsibility for his actions is a thematic constant in Branner's corpus which may be traced back even to his earliest works. The weak person exerts his personal freedom by committing some act, but when placed under attack for its consequences he desires punishment and lacks the courage and inner conviction to defend his initial act. He neurotically hides away from life and adopts the posture of a petulant child with his demands for restrictive punishment. For such neurotic individuals personal security takes the form of punitive unhappiness. This interpretaton would seem to clarify Hans Egge's superficially cryptic remark in *Eftermæle* that Cæcilie "lacked security. She first found it again after she was beaten and had become unhappy." The lack of punitive response for the active expression of personal freedom creates the psychological complexities of its dilemma. The weak person can only learn to identify his personal freedom through punitive confinement, and his weakness is defined as his inability to accept the responsibility for the consequences of his actions. He cannot assure himself of a meaningful moral freedom, because its realization is denied by his dependency on punitive condemnation, the price he pays for disengagement from moral responsibility. This is the ethical superstructure of the dramatic impact which *Skibet* and *De blaa Undulater* convey; it is this superstructure which places these seemingly insignificant events in a larger, universal perspective and causes us to reflect upon them long after a first reading.

Ingeborg[19] has all the pathos and charm of H. C. Andersen's *Little Match Girl*. Like *Iris* it is the story of confrontation between a lower-class girl and an upper-class girl. Ingeborg treasures her ragged and tattered doll, Ruth. It is her most beloved possession. One day before Christmas she meets Annelise Seidelin and her mother outside a toy shop. Poor Ingeborg has been standing and staring longingly at the marvelous dolls inside, and Annelise's mother actually buys one for Ingeborg. Bewildered and amazed, Ingeborg decides that she must reciprocate with an equivalent show of kindness, and so she gives Ruth to Annelise. However, the new doll is not Ruth, but Annelise, and can hardly take Ruth's place. When Annelise returns Ruth in disgust, Ingeborg is crushed and, attempting to rid herself of an unspeakable hurt, she throws the doll out of the window.

In *Drenge om Foraaret*[20] we again meet a boy named Börge who is awakened to the implications of sexuality. Börge's playmate, Jakob, like Katrine, is the child of a broken home. Jakob says that he will loan Börge his water pistol if Börge will shoot the first adult who comes along. He shoots an elderly lady—violence. He then lies to his mother and says that the whole affair was Jakob's fault—lying. Once again we are presented with two fundamental elements of Branner's stories of childhood: guilt and responsibility.

De tre Musketerer[21] is another story of puberty and affords us a glimpse of a rare moment of high comedy in Branner's writing. The three musketeers are three twelve-year-old boys who are united in their love—hate for a noble lady, alias Mussy Mortensen. They are sworn to destroy Mussy Mortensen as a temptress and plot to steal her picture from the front window of a photography shop. Their adventure culminates at the police station, where they bravely confront the law:

> He said it with a sharp glitter in his gold-rimmed glasses, and finally asked Johan if it was true that he'd have burned the photo of the young lady?
> "Yes," Johan said.
> "Well, but why? That you might want to steal it I can understand. But burn it? What was the motive?"
> Athos cleared his throat. "I wanted to prevent this woman from driving unstable souls into misery," he said.[22]

Röde Heste i Sneen[23] is yet another story about young love. While sledding with a classmate, fifteen year old Niels topples over and his beloved falls on top of him and kisses him. The reality of sexuality has suddenly struck him, and he repeatedly reflects upon the experience as he trudges homeward with his sled. He feels himself marked for death by the only thing which had ever happened in his life. The sexual urge is epitomized as a sort of primitive life force so powerful that to deny it is to embrace death. In *Röde Heste i Sneen*, as well as elsewhere in Branner, the influence of Frank Wedekind is quite obvious, and Branner freely admitted to having been greatly influenced by the German expressionist.[24] The emphasis on the awakening of sensuality and the paring to essentials of the elements of conflict, unencumbered by detail, as well as the dreamlike narrative tone from which those elements take their sustenance, all point toward that influence.

Röde Heste i Sneen is immediately followed by *Den förste Morgen*,[25] the story of a man's love on the morning after his wedding night in a hotel in Hälsingborg. As in the foregoing story, the protagonist experiences the awakening of a new life within himself as the result of contact with the creative principle of love. Finally, the couple wander into a churchyard and stand before an inscription on one of the gravestones which reads: "Let us remember how few are our days," which recalls the theme of *Om lidt er vi borte*. His new position in life has transformed him and he is no longer alone, for everything about him has come to life as a result of "her" sharing his existence with him. Like Niels Rude in *Drömmen om en Kvinde*, they are to play together, to make a game of reality and reality a game:

"Yes, but can't you understand me," he said and pursued her across the corridor and into her room, into her dancing sun. "You're part of the games I played as a boy. It's reality that is nonsense. Play is reality. We're going to play with each other, that's why we have each other. The world is full of people who have forgotten how to play. The world is full of dead adults. The world is full of solemn and monstrous adults. . . ."[26]

In *Shagpiben*[27] a woman returns from the hospital where she has just watched her husband die. The story is related as a stream of consciousness as she reflects on the meaning of things in people's lives. She considers the objects in the house which remind her of her life together with her husband. Finally, her attention is attracted to the pipe which they had once both admired in a shop window and which she had bought for him. When the stream of consciousness has run full course and her reflections have transformed her by giving her a new vision of reality, she changes her attitude toward death. The "no" she uttered at the hospital is now answered by a vigorous "yes," a yes saying to both life and death.

Emil Frederiksen has pointed out that Branner wrote this story while still at work on *Drömmen om en Kvinde* and that the widow's attitude toward material objects recalls Knud Mortimer's and Mimi Fleischer's attitude toward things.[28] She sees that objects do not change, but only stand and wait: life merely stands and waits for us to accept it or deny it, while it simultaneously goes rushing on:

But she didn't fall and she didn't look up either, for she knew that a coat was there somewhere, waiting for her. And a walking stick was waiting for her, and a hat; the whole house was full of things that were silent and waiting.[29]

Ægteskab[30] is a story of young love gone wrong. Johannes's marriage is about to go on the rocks, and he and his wife barely speak to each other. While pondering asking for a divorce, he visits his former schoolmaster in his home village. He then discovers that the schoolmaster has lived together with his wife for years without having spoken to her. They have nearly driven one another mad. Having viewed marital cruelty and chaos at close range, Johannes turns to the schoolmaster and, as Jörn Vosmar asserts,[31] utters the message which lies hidden in many of Branner's stories about couples:

"Don't you know that that's why a man and a woman have each other—so that they won't be driven mad by loneliness?" [32]

Johannes then flees home on the train to his wife and hopes that she will stay with him. He presses close to the dew covered train window and says: "Stay with me," and his whispered plea recalls the tone of *Om lidt er vi borte*.

To Minutters Stilhed [33] is a highly concentrated version of the earlier story with the same name. Tidemand, the merchant, stands beside his wife's deathbed and struggles to recall the time when the drive for money, power, and prestige had not yet made his marriage meaningless. He discovers that these pursuits had completely occupied him and he had consequently lost contact with his wife. Now that she is dead, he no longer recognizes her. Unlike the nameless widow in *Shagpiben*, his intense reflections do not have the power to transform him, to recast him as a sensitive being. Tidemand, in precisely the same manner as Skjold-Lassen in the earlier version of the story, is incapable of growth and spiritual development. When he greets the first visitor who comes to offer condolences, he slips back into the role of the conventional bourgeois merchant. His words to the visitor are only slightly different from those of Skjold-Lassen:

"Thanks, Carl, that you came. You have no idea what it means to me that precisely you are the first person I meet after Ragna . . . after Ragna has died." [34]

In *Sidst i August*[35] we meet a couple who have missed something in the ten years they have been married. They have begun to lose contact with each other, and they have romantically set out on a trip to see "the mountains." For them the mountains symbolize the never-never land of fantastic happiness, something inaccessible and unobtainable which will imaginatively restore and renew their love. They become stranded in Paris as the war breaks out, and they never reach the mountains. They have become so immersed in one another that they are incapable of realizing that they have individual qualities and demands. They have quite simply become blind to their individual identities. This impression is stylistically conveyed by the story's being essentially told in a "we" point of view. Only sporadically is the

The Art of the Short Story

husband able to disassociate himself from his wife, Winnie, and realize her as an individual, which is indicated by a shift to the first person. The collective puts their fates into perspective: they represent the immediate prewar generation which had lost a sense of identity and which was to be collectively hurtled along the path to oblivion in the holocaust that was to follow. During their wandering through Paris they observe signs of the impending crisis, but they also note that no one seems to be overly concerned. They listen as a Danish travel agent assures a Swedish tourist that war will never come. They watch as people still gather and sit complacently at Café de la Paix. Winnie bursts into tears on the street, but no one takes any notice of her. A general lack of human contact and concern reigns over all as they steadily grow closer and closer together. The strain of anticipating the dreadful events which are to come has forced them to reevaluate each other and has given them a need for "togetherness." Finally, they are to take the last boat home from Antwerp. On their last night in Paris they climb to the top of Montmartre and look down at the city below:

"Well, we didn't reach the mountains," I said.
Winnie's face was empty and white in the dark, her voice sounded tired.
"Isn't it just the same," she said. "Isn't it just the same now whether you and I get to see the mountains or not." [36]

Their dream of the mountains has lost its urgency, for the emotional force engendered by anticipating the war has reduced their private aspirations to something insignificant and forced them together once more as sensitive individuals.

In 1939 Branner wrote a short sketch entitled, *Sidste Skib*,[37] which is essentially the same story as *Sidst i August*. It is another "we" story of a couple who leave Paris at the last moment in order to return home, but it lacks the thematic and symbolic unity of *Sidst i August*. The unifying symbol of the mountains and the note of necessity for mutual contact and understanding we find in *Sidst i August* are lacking here. This story is probably a preliminary sketch for *Sidst i August* and, as such, it may offer insight into Branner's working methods. *Sidste Skib* presents the same situation as we find in *Sidst i August*, but it is told in a flat, journalistic style. Given the situation and the descriptions of complacency and unconcern of the boat passengers in *Sidste Skib,* Branner may then have revised the earlier story and infused it with the symbolism and unifying theme of a couple's rapprochement. From this comparison we may conclude that Branner generally sketched a situation and then wrote a draft in fairly pedestrian form. He then proceeded to fill out his canvas with a penetrating analysis of human relations and, with a few deft strokes, embellished it with a symbolic superstructure to epitomize the story's thematic and effective properties.

There appears to be a certain thematic dichotomy which separates the two collections *Om lidt er vi borte* and *To Minutters Stilhed.* In the earlier collection people are confronted with a variety of crises, crises which they attempt to resolve; and these stories may be loosely and generally characterized as tales of crisis–conflict–resolution. In the second collection, however, most of the stories appear to be variations on the themes of love and the necessity for human contact, the very problems treated in the last story from which the collection takes its title. We have the awakening of love in *Drenge om Foraaret* and *Röde Heste i Sneen.* In *Den förste Morgen* we see the nascent stages of marital love, while in *Ægteskab* we see that same love gone sour. In *Shagpiben* and *To Minutters Stilhed* we see how death often necessitates a reevaluation of the meaning of love, and finally in *Sidst i August* we see how a love relegated to an unobtainable fantasy can be circumstantially transformed into a meaningful reality.

Certainly *Om lidt er vi borte* and *To Minutters Stilhed* contain the best of Branner's short stories through 1944, and our discussion so far has shown how he developed into a master photographer of the brief, meaningful moment in a person's life and how that moment attains universal importance when thrown into a wider perspective. In addition to the stories contained in these collections, together with those contained in Sunday supplements, there are a few other stories from this period which, although they are not representative of the best of his craftsmanship, at least deserve honorable mention. One of these is *En halv Alen Vand.*[38]

En halv Alen Vand tells of two lovers, Christen and Anne. Anne is an unsuccessful nightclub singer and Christen is her camp follower. Both are penniless and abandon their hotel to avoid paying the bill. They then have no money to eat or to leave the village, and Anne finally suggests that they sleep in the cottage of a man who once gave her two hundred crowns. Christen then discovers that she had received the money for sleeping with the man, and he decides that he will commit suicide by jumping off a bridge. He discovers that there are only three feet of water beneath the bridge. Anne runs after him, finds that he has not jumped, and then bursts out laughing when she discovers why. In spite of her infidelity and their financial status, they still have each other.

Grænselandet[39] is set in war-torn China during the Japanese invasion. Two war correspondents and a priest are seated at the bottom of a bunker, where they are methodically counting the intervals of silence between incoming shells. A Chinese soldier sitting near them is shot, and they look on as he dies. Father Nebel, the missionary, as well as the other two correspondents are all well acquainted with the horrors of war, and their personal lives concern them far more deeply.

We have now discussed all of Branner's short stories through 1944 with the exception of *Katten*.[40] In 1945 Branner wrote a lyrical story about a poet and his love for a young girl which appeared in a limited edition as a Christmas gift from the Copenhagen publishing firm of Carit Andersen.[41] For the poet, the young girl is his dream of a woman, yet he feels that she hampers him in his work. For him she must remain a dream. At times, he concludes, it is necessary to have a fantastic dream of love rather than a reality, and it is only when she has gone that he misses her.

Though not a short story, it is perhaps fitting at this point to discuss Branner's third radio play, *Natteregn*,[42] for it has many of the themes that we find in the collection *To Minutters Stilhed*. *Natteregn* recounts a couple's life in the form of nocturnal vignettes. There are only two nameless characters: He and She, and we follow them for a period of 35–40 years. When the play opens they are a young couple deeply in love, and he says:

"I swear that I shall live and die with you, and I shall always be true to you. Always, do you hear." [43]

They laugh and believe that they are the only couple to have experienced love so deeply. He swears that he will never assume the role of a fat, lethargic "slipper hero." We next look in on them two years later, and the blossom has already gone off their pristine love. He has been unfaithful, but their wounds are bound up and they go on. Three years later we see them once more as they are discussing how sick their baby is. Their love has now turned to companionship, a friendship to combat loneliness, and she utters the same plea as the wife in *Om lidt er vi borte*:

"Then take my hand—take hold of my hand. Let me feel that you believe it. —You don't believe it at all." [44]

He is still able to fantasize, and, like the man we meet in *Sidst i August* and later in *Et Spil om Kærligheden og Döden*, he conjures up the image of a trip to a distant land in the hope that escapist fantasy will restore and renew their love:

"Now we're on board the ship, can you see that? —We've already been sailing for many days and nights. And now it's evening, and we're sitting on the deck and staring at the stars." [45]

Ten years later we meet them after they have just had a party, and their love has gone totally sour. Their souls have died in a quest for materialism:

He: Yes, it speaks to us, but we don't understand it.
(Pause. —Music)
I believe we're dead people, you and I.
She: What sort of nonsense is that.
He: We just don't realize it, because it's happened little by little, and we haven't noticed it. But someday when we knock at Heaven's gate, then Saint Peter will look out at us and ask: "Where are your souls?—Don't you have any souls?—No, you don't have any souls. You must have lost them somewhere. Go back and find them." [46]

A myopic vision of the meaningful values in life has created a gulf between them, and He has become everything which disgusted Him at the outset, one of the "slipper heroes" whose search for materialistic values alone has frozen his sensibility.

Following this scene is an intermezzo which relates the man's conversation with his mistress. She claims that she loves him and urges him to leave his wife and flee with her to his summer house. She soon discovers that he is weak willed and will not give up his wife, for she has become a habit:

She: Yes, you enjoy your own weakness. And now I don't want to hear any more about your marriage, do you understand. I'm asking you for the last time: will you come with me, or are you going to remain with her? [47]

In the final scene we see the couple after an interval of twenty years. They are now in the autumn of life, and their love has turned into a mutual caring for each other's petty concerns, such as whether or not he is cold, or whether or not she can sleep. He has dreamt that he has died, and when he gets to heaven, Saint Peter refuses to admit him because he has no Order of the Garter. Some thirty years earlier he had not been admitted because his soul had died, but now a testimonial for having lived in accordance with the rules is more important than a soul. His dream of love has been killed by the exigencies of sterile rules. His transition into the character that he abhorred at the outset has been just as steady as the rain which has pattered outside throughout every scene. At the outset, like Claus Böje in *Barnet leger ved Stranden* and Niels Rude in *Drömmen om en Kvinde*, he has believed in a dream of love. He has then struggled to recapture that dream and finally he has lost sight of the dream and succumbed to a habitual acquaintance with someone he formerly loved. Once more Branner is saying that as soon as the fantasy and infatuation of love has disappeared, then love is transformed into something which deadens its very soul.

In their compressed and connected format the vignettes in *Natteregn* cover the whole gambit of marital love, and in tone they remind one very much of Sigurd Hoel's *Möte ved milepelen* and *En dag i oktober,* where characters are easily dehumanized by their failure to acept the fantasy of love and permit its galactic power to enrich their lives. They lose sight of life's objectives when they become entangled in a pursuit of their own petty goals. In the process spontaneous emotional expression is transformed into mechanical rigidity. The resolution of the conflict between the two poles of this transformation was one of Branner's major concerns during the 1930s, but it was also to occupy his artistic vision in his later works.

Branner's short stories provided a source of influence and inspiration for younger Danish authors, and this is clearly seen in the short stories of Peer Schaldemose, Erik Dreyer and Finn Gerdes.

It is interesting to note that Finn Gerdes has written a short story, *En Dreng og en Ring* in the collection *De blaa Gardiner* (1943), which in title and contents is very reminiscent of Branner.

Had Branner's career ended with his early works, he would have been assured of a prominent position in Danish letters, but he might never have achieved whatever international acclaim he subsequently received. It is significant to note that none of his novels from this period (*Legetöj, Barnet leger ved Stranden, Drömmen om en Kvinde, Historien om Börge*) has been translated into English, whereas selected short stories from this period have recently appeared in English under the title *Two Minutes of Silence* (1966), a translation which loses the intended symbolic meaning. The reference was to the two minutes of silence observed on November 11 as a silent prayer for peace, and the collection was originally displayed in shop windows as a form of protest during the darkest days of the German Occupation. Branner had not taken an active part in the Danish Resistance. His personal indecision on this matter led to a crisis of conscience which is reflected in *Trommerne* and *Angst,* books which belong to the next period of his career as a dramatist of the soul, for they contain many of the stylistic devices he was to employ in *Rytteren* and *Ingen kender Natten,* perhaps the two major achievements of his career.

We have subjected early works of Branner's career to a thorough analysis in order to uncover the very roots of the thematic, structural, and symbolic devices he was to employ so effectively in both his earlier and his later works. Branner grew as a craftsman, but his esthetic vision remained unchanged. Branner's major technical accomplishment in his short stories had been the refined use of dialogue, repetitive imagery, and parallel situations. Now he was to turn briefly to the theater, and it seems clear that Branner, like Henry James, remained a frustrated playwright. He lacked a dynamic sense of the dramatic—a clear view of the physical emergence and interaction of character. However, he was to produce only three stage plays, and of these, *Söskende,* the least original dramatically, merits the greatest praise. Just four years before his death, Branner wrote an encomium for the playwright Kjeld Abell, a contemporary who had belatedly become a friend.[48] There Branner reveals as much about himself as about Kjeld

Abell. He states that Abell resorted to masks and guises, a thing he could never do himself, and consequently Branner's stage characters stand naked as conceptual exponents and are dramatically unreal.

CHAPTER 4

Dramatic Interlude

IN 1942 Branner contributed an essay–short story, *Trommerne,* to a collection entitled *Ny Nordisk Novellekunst*.[1] *Trommerne* is, as Johan Borgen has said of *Bjergene,* "a piece of bleeding personal admission, one of the most daring pieces of literature I know."[2] It might well be summarized in philosophical terms as a psychic disquisition on exculpation. It is the monologue of an author's anxious ego addressed to the wife with whom he had lost contact. The drums symbolize the cacophony of war in the background and, as Emil Frederiksen says: "the eye of the needle, *i.e.* the situation into which the story's narrator feels himself forced,"[3] a situation in which the narrator does what he feels he must do: believe in something, in God, in humanity, in a multifarious life, in a meaning of the whole.

The anonymous "I" of *Trommerne* is in the midst of an emotional crisis. He has lost faith in the efficacy of an author's self-imposed purpose to present reality, hope, and conviction in times of moral chaos. The question of *Trommerne* is, then, the universal one of the ability of the poet as the servant of his community and its effective spokesman to awaken that community to the necessity of moral conviction. First, the poet must convince himself of the priority of this end and that he is not reprehensible in comparison with those who perhaps suffer less spiritually but are in greater physical danger, for they may lose their lives by actively resisting. The poet must exculpate himself from the crime of silence in a time of moral crisis. His anxiety results from his inability to speak out effectively. As a result of his anguish, the poet feels that his message has become disjunctive and meaningless:

> I read over what I had written and found even better words for it. I crossed out and corrected and made additions. I read it over again and corrected it again. Now the page was a complete labyrinth of de-

Dramatic Interlude

letions and additions and brackets and marginal comments and long arrows which twisted in and out between the lines to show that this should be replaced by that and that that should stand for this. When I was to read it for the third time, I could no longer find any coherence in it—the entire thing had dissolved into sentences, and the sentences into words, and the words into small black marks on paper.[4]

Like Claus Böje in *Barnet leger ved Stranden* who can only find typographical errors in the detective novels he reads, the author's unity of thought has dissolved in anguish, so that he can only see meaningless details and cannot impose a pattern of meaning upon the totality of existence.

In *Trommerne* Branner shows that, in order to rid himself of anxiety, the poet must recognize the source of his anxiety. Branner therefore presents the most elementary of the Freudian dicta: the recognition of the cause of mental disorder is the first step in overcoming it. In a letter to Johan Borgen, Branner makes it clear that one of the major functions of the modern author is to indicate the source of our anxieties:

When schizophrenia has spread so far and penetrated so deeply into our renowned Western culture that it is no longer regarded as schizophrenia, but as an integral part of the normal person's being, then it is up to the abnormal artist alone to make us conscious of the disease and recreate identity.[5]

Having outlined the nature of his problem, the self-conscious narrator of *Trommerne* embarks upon a quest, a sort of Pilgrim's Progress of the soul. Pressed to the brink of despair and with the sound of militant drums resounding in his ears, he attempts to pass through the eye of the needle of belief in order to make us aware of that disease and recreate spiritual identity:

I had never seen anything in the world before I saw that wall. I look and look and recognize it. All my life I've been on the way toward that wall. Now I'm already standing with my back against it, and the sound of the drums drowns out everything. Now I'm looking directly into the gun barrel's small black holes—that's my needle's eye. I no longer have control over my life.[6]

The intensity of realistic illusion is complete. He then wanders off through the Kafkaesque nightmare that is the occupied city.

Voices become audible and then fade against the backdrop of drums. From this truncated vision, later greatly expanded in *Angst*, the author emerges from the city at dawn and pauses to stare at the sky:

> But clear out over the flat horizon the cloud bank lifted its leaden lid a moment and I saw a bluish green strip of sky loom forth. Finally, I saw nothing else but that. I looked into a world which was infinitely far off, but a world of clarity and peace.[7]

He has finally seen the light at the end of the long tunnel of despair and absolved himself of anxiety. Should his wife return, he promises to place his head in her lap and remain silent. He has seen a vision of hope and wishes to regain contact with humanity. His vision of light is strikingly similar to the vision which Knud Mortimer and Merete Rude see at the conclusions of the cathedral scenes in *Drömmen om en Kvinde*. Contextually different as the cathedral scenes and the "horizon" scene in *Trommerne* certainly are, they are thematically the same: the limits of hope are extended so that a search for human contact can be made.[8]

In *Angst*,[9] an expanded and altered version of *Trommerne*, subtle changes are made in the concluding "horizon" scenes. Compare the passage in *Trommerne* with the corresponding passage below from *Angst*:

> But clear out over the flat horizon the cloud bank lifted its leaden lid, and a strip of bluish green morning sky loomed forth. It lasted only an instant, then it disappeared again, but I kept seeing it before me and finally I saw nothing else but that.[10]

The vision of the world of clarity and peace has been deleted in *Angst*. Note, too, the effect of the final sentence, which makes it seem that the vision of peace and hope had been present all the time (*then it disappeared again*), but the mental disorder of the observing narrator has merely blinded him to it. The cathedral scenes in *Drömmen om en Kvinde,* the horizon scenes in *Trommerne* and *Angst,* and the concluding passages of *Barnet leger ved Stranden, Ingen kender Natten* and *Dæmoner ved Daggry* offer an excellent example of the kaleidoscopic aspect of Branner's technique. He often places similar scenes in decidedly different contexts to gain altogether different effects. An image assumes different significance each time it is twisted and turned within a radically different context, and Branner's gallery of imaginative exponents thereby takes on the quality of movable segments in a collage. The gallery must be observed in its entirety before a specific meaning can be associated with any of its parts.

In addition to stylistic differences of the sort we have just noted, there are other important differences between *Trommerne* and *Angst*. In both an author is writing to his wife. In the former we are given little factual information about her, while in the latter we are told that she is a Jewess, which, in light of the World War II background, adds poignancy. In *Angst* the narrator tells us that he is writing a play, while in *Trommerne* we are merely told that he is an author. In *Angst*, but not in *Trommerne*, the narrator quotes Christ's words to Saint Peter in the garden. Though no Christ-figure identification was probably intended, the narrator's quotation shows us that he has realized that his mission as a poet is to awaken his sleeping countrymen in a time of crisis. Chiefly, however, it is the quest sequence, the narrator's wanderings through the occupied city at night, which is greatly expanded in *Angst*. In this sequence the narrator meets a child who is leaning against a lamp post. He is beating a toy bucket and singing a monotonous song in an incomprehensible language. The child disappears as the lamp flicks off. He sees a bored man on a train reading news of the war. He overhears a crowd discussing how fortunate they are that they can still get decent pastry. A couple walks by and then the two people part as the man says that he will never meet the girl again. He discovers a room filled with people standing with their arms raised above their heads. When someone touches them, the spell is broken, and they laugh. And thus the sequence of nightmarish incidents proceeds. Every time the narrator is on the brink of approaching those whom he sees, of taking part in their games and questioning them, they disappear. Reality is thereby defined as a sequence of terrifying dreams populated by characters who evaporate whenever an observer attempts to contact them. The observer is nameless, as are the actors in the series of dream-dramas he observes. He attempts to write his name, to say it, but he fails. He has lost his identity. A woman he meets refuses to give him her name. She, like the narrator and all those whom he meets, is an anonymous robot caught up in what is at once both a ridiculous and terrifying game devoid of human contact and sympathy. The narrator is reduced to a passive observer. In his passivity he is like the immobile Tomas in *Ingen kender Natten* who cannot rise to act. Like Tomas, he must follow the lonely path through the eye of the needle of faith in order to discover and accept an "other directed" sense of communal responsibility. At the outset, like Tomas, he cannot distinguish between reality and fantasy. He begins his quest in a state in which he:

". . . no longer knows what is dream and what is reality. I don't know if it is my dreams which create reality of themselves, or if it is reality which approaches from afar and penetrates my waking sleep.[11]

Finally, he ends his quest by recognizing a vision of hope, and the spell of illusory anxiety is broken. The truth has been found not in artistic concepts, but in the reality of artistic activity. The disillusioned author began by questioning the efficacy of his craft in an hour of crisis:

But how will he tell others about the shining world that he alone has seen? Can it help to talk to the white smock who writes down crazy Latin words in his journal, to the tramping boots and the jingling bunch of keys? [12]

The narrator hated his own words, grew ashamed of himself as an artist and subsequently lost his wife, all as the result of his inability to take an active part in accepting the responsibility of the intellectual.

The truth for which the author is searching is commonplace enough. He is, as we suggested at the outset, searching for the answer to a universal question: can a poet believe in his ability to present reality and convey hope and conviction in times of crisis? Does he have the courage and creative power to achieve a Socratic victory when it is demanded of him? Obviously, there is nothing more boring than the novelist-hero in search of himself, for the non-novelist reader can hardly share the intensely personal doubts of a novelist-hero about his own creative power. There are innumerable failures and few successes in this genre. It is only when the motivations of the "autobiographical" artist are related

Dramatic Interlude

to the attempt of the reader to test out in his own experience the possibility of a new conceptual and esthetic form which will give him imaginative grasp of his world that attempts in this genre achieve success, such as *A la recherche du temps perdu* and *A Portrait of the Artist as a Young Man*. If autobiographical and essentially artistic concerns are coupled with the attempt to find a valid order of reality, one which will relate his artistic function with the rest of life, then such autobiographical studies take on significance for everyone in the here and now. In times of cultural crisis it is not only the artist who has a spiritual need to commit himself to a quest into his personal life to find in it a meaningful pattern, a direction, that corresponds to his feelings, but it is the concern of every thinking and feeling man. In order for that concern to be related to the reader a bond must be erected between the reader and the artist, and their concerns must clearly dovetail.

Trommerne and *Angst* are not failures, though both are far removed from Branner's major successes. How he averts failure is perhaps the most crucial problem in a discussion of these works, and the answer lies in a careful analysis of his technique. First, the effects of deliberate confusion of the kind we encounter in *Angst* and *Trommerne* demand complete communion between the author-narrator and the reader. Only then can the introspective discoveries made by the author-narrator appear to be made by the reader and thus take on significance. Control of sympathy, a delicate matter, is a means of establishing this communion, and it is accomplished at the very outset in both *Trommerne* and *Angst*. The author-narrator addresses himself directly to the reader in a tone of self-conscious desperation, and a sense of a communal bond evolves. Compare, for example, the opening paragraphs of *Trommerne* and *Angst*:

Trommerne
I can't write to you, because each time I begin to write I forget what really matters in order to make it sound nice and credible, and in that way I don't get anywhere with you. You know reality all too well.[13]

Angst
Besides that wouldn't suffice, because each time I begin to write I forget what really matters in order to make it sound nice and credible, and I know that I won't get anywhere by lying to you.[14]

The line: "You know reality all too well" in *Trommerne* is deleted in *Angst* and replaced by: "by lying to you." The change was probably made in the interest of furthering the bond between the reader and the author-narrator. The reader asks: How could he know that I know reality all too well? He is certain in *Angst* however, that the author-narrator is embarking upon an honest confession. The list of examples of similar changes between the two works could be extended, but this serves to indicate the sort of stylistic changes that were made, and the sum total of these alterations effectively establishes a sense of communion between reader and author-narrator.

Once the bond of identity is established, the reader is forced to regard the author-narrator's dilemma as his own. The narrator is writing directly to me, the reader thinks, and he does not have a clear conceptual pattern of life and art, but do I? The subject of *Trommerne* and *Angst* becomes something which everyone experiences, whether he realizes it or not: an intellectual quest for some kind of truth about reality. Most important for establishing this bond of recognition is the author-narrator's estrangement from his wife. This is the rhetorical device by which he is realistically permitted to address himself directly to us. Then, too, his use of the war as a sort of "objective correlative" makes the reader fully aware of the seriousness and relevance of the author-narrator's dilemma, and it provides a concrete background with which the reader can readily identify. The final sections of both stories serve to show us just how difficult it is to distinguish between reality and fantasy: they mark a disturbing disclosure of the failure of the social environment as a trustworthy carrier of recognizable ethical and moral values. Consequently, they indicate just how difficult the task is to awaken others to the necessity of accepting ethical imperatives when the very reality of those imperatives is called into question. These, then, are some of the techniques Branner uses in *Angst* and *Trommerne,* and it is clear that the technical, procedural aspect of his craftsmanship is here united with the message he wishes to convey, and that is the critical necessity of accepting ethical imperatives, the imperative to redefine one's view of reality in a time of cultural crisis. His technique permits a keen sense of identification with the author-narrator's dilemma, and his problems, as they become related to our own, take on a new significance. His personal quest becomes a

Dramatic Interlude

universal quest for identification. It is strongly reminiscent of Claus Böje's quest in *Barnet leger ved Stranden*. However, as Jörn Vosmar suggests:

> . . . it is a long way from *Barnet leger ved Stranden*, where weakness was exclusively a sign of sexual failure, to *Angst*, where Branner—simultaneously with Martin A. Hansen—has discovered that power which can conceal itself behind weakness, a mysterium which he elaborates upon in *Rytteren*.[15]

On December 8, 1949, Branner published what is generally considered to be one of his most controversial books, the novel *Rytteren*. Originally conceived as a short story,[16] *Rytteren* takes place during a period of, roughly speaking, eighteen hours, and it is divided into segments or acts: *morning, noon, afternoon, evening,* and *night.* The action is largely centered around three people: Clemens, a metropolitan doctor, Susanne, his mistress, and Hubert, a riding master who was kicked to death by a horse. Hubert, though dead when the novel opens, has such a hold on the living that he may actually be considered one of the active participants. Both Susanne and Clemens are deeply disturbed by Hubert's death, and, via the retrospective method, their lives are extended back in time so that we discover why they are so troubled by his death. We are then permitted to follow along with them as they rid themselves of the haunting specter of the dead Hubert.

When first published *Rytteren* was hailed by a chorus of enthusiastic critics as a masterpiece and the crowning achievement of Branner's career. As time passed, however, opinion shifted to judge Clemens as the book's central character, and many critics asserted that his vacillating weakness and guilt made him unsuitable as the ideal of an important piece of literature. It was also objected that his characterization as a clown made him an unsuitable spokesman for the venerable humanistic ideals he was presumed to represent. Then, too, it was asserted that the novella was too architectually planned, too rigid, and that its contrapuntal counterbalancing of characters directed the reader's attention away from its imposing thematic and effectual qualities to its structure. In short, *Rytteren* soon became the subject of a heated critical controversy, and for the first time Branner's following became something more than a mere coterie of intimates. In his review the noted critic and author Tom Kristensen asserted that, had the novel been written in English, Branner would have become a famous man.[17] Hans Brix contended that the novel's central question was the simplistic one of who killed Hubert, thereby dismissing the work as a sort of detective novel, and he suggested that it was Susanne, as Clemens suggests.[18] Ten days after *Rytteren* appeared, Branner was interviewed by *Nationaltidende* and asked to give his own interpretation. Branner replied that many critics had misinterpreted Clemens as a weak character, whereas he had intended Clemens to stand as a portrait of human frailty and strength. Concerning the work's central conflict, Branner stated that initially he had been interested in the erotic theme alone, but had finally centered the conflict around a woman who is emotionally restricted to a dead man and cannot, therefore, relate to one who is alive. When questioned whether or not he had been influenced by Kafka, Branner responded that Kafka represented an isolated phenomenon and did not provide a substantial basis for sustained influence.[19] However, he continued to state that James Joyce had perhaps spoiled the work, for the use of inner monologue easily led him to complete formlessness necessarily terminating in chaos, but he added that he exerted discipline in the dialogues.

The critical controversy pro and con surrounding *Rytteren* raged on for more than a year after its appearance. Niels Kaas Johansen categorized Susanne as a refined middle-class matron and questioned whether or not she had the inner psychic power to be transformed as she was.[20] Kaas Johansen was content to merely question the realia behind the novel's thematic details while overlooking Branner's avowed purpose: to awaken people to the enormity of the responsibility involved in being human.[21] Johansen's article itself was viewed as controversial and was answered by Bergliot Nielsen who, posing as an "ordinary" reader, contended that the novel was a chapter in the eternal battle between the forces of good and evil in which good—in the form of Clemens—won out.[22]

This brief and partial recapitulation of the critical controversy surrounding *Rytteren* indicates the important position it soon occupied in contemporary Danish literature. As always when craftsmanship and intent are called into question and an author's work

Dramatic Interlude

evokes violently opposed superlatives, it is an expression of the work's complexity and not infrequently that it is of lasting value. In any review of critical commentary on this novel it is most significant to note that *Rytteren* was subjected to the critical eye of one of Branner's foremost contemporaries, Karen Blixen, whose copy of the novel at Rungstedlund is filled with innumerable pencil marks, figures and marginal notes, indicating that she had made a thorough study of it. Karen Blixen had long been concerned with Branner's work, and, after a bit of literary detective work, Thorkild Björnvig has uncovered a damning comment by that authoress on Branner's mode of characterization—with particular reference to *Rytteren:*

> While Karen Blixen means that, if the characters themselves "shall form and determine the story," then it will, like an all too human and not a divine art—"end by evaporating and becoming nothing." (*Sidste Fortællinger*, 27). But this is actually a piece of modern literary criticism placed in the Cardinal's mouth. . . . The Cardinal's replique applies in particular to H. C. Branner's short stories and novels.[23]

For Karen Blixen the art of the storyteller was divine, and her tales are embroidered with the style and subtlety of classical myth and punctuated with the message that simple humanism is not enough. In her marionette dramas it is the storyteller, not the character, who controls the evolution of character, and she clearly considered the exegesis of her craft as diametrically opposed to that of Branner. The storyteller constructs myth from a symbolic, outer view of life, while Branner views life symbolically through the forceful fabrication of images, such as the unifying image of the horse in *Rytteren*. Karen Blixen's images are not sterile symbols, but viable mythical entities. Her *Weltanschauung* was essentially Elizabethan in its general conception of a world order with every part subordinated to an overall pattern. It is the view enunciated by Ulysses in his speech on "degree" in *Troilus and Cressida*, for it is the view of an indivisible cosmic order.[24] Whereas Karen Blixen's images have their natural setting in the age-old folk tale, Branner's use of symbols is entirely modern in conception and purpose. The horse as symbol in *Rytteren* is an emotional correlative and is functionally the same as the soldier's well in Aage Dons's *Soldaterbrönden* (1936), where characterization is impoverished if the organizational and thematic importance of the well as symbol is removed. Karen Blixen's outlook is essentially aristocratic, for individual sovereignty and freedom are magical principles, not goals to be consciously attained, as they form an inherent mode of existence. Branner's view is, of course, the antithesis of this, but Hubert may be considered a mythical aristocrat, for he is conceived as a totally free being who exists solely in the memories of those who knew him. He represents the personified force of nature "in the time before original sin, a time when horses wandered freely over misty plains." [25] He is the vision of nature as a morally blind force.

Although *Rytteren* has frequently been subjected to careful analysis and although Karen Blixen and H. C. Branner did not share the same critical and artistic views, Karen Blixen's essay remains the most thorough and pentrating analysis of the novel to date. Her essay was written in 1949, but was not intended for publication, and it was not until many years later that it appeared together with a short epilogue.[26] Her essay is a most perceptive analysis in which she indicates problems and interpretive possibilities which had eluded the professional critics. Steen Eiler Rasmussen[27] has convincingly pointed out just how concerned she must have been with *Rytteren* and suggests that she conceived *Spögelseshestene* as her poetic answer to *Rytteren*. *Spögelseshestene* was read over Danmarks Radio on December 15, 1950, little more than a year after the publication of *Rytteren,* but her story was apparently written before *Rytteren* appeared.[28] *Spögelseshestene* is remarkable as the only one of Karen Blixen's tales to have a contemporary setting, and the similarities with *Rytteren* are striking, though there are distinct differences. In her story Billy is the counterpart of Hubert and is dead when the story begins. Susanne's counterpart is Nonny, and Clemens's is the young painter Cedric, but Billy and Nonny are children—Billy is ten and Nonny is six. Karen Blixen's *Rytteren* has the setting of *Historien om Börge,* but the central themes of both *Rytteren and Spögelseshestene* are the same. Susanne and Nonny are emotionally tied to dead men and can neither respond nor relate to a living person. In his enlightening comparison of these two stories, Steen Eiler Rasmussen[29] points out that, whereas Hubert represents animalistic nature, Billy is an exponent of tradition and culture, the riding master before the Fall and, in significant contrast to Hubert, he is an artist, a creative teller of tales. While Clemens is the beneficent savior and symbol of goodness, Cedric is an artist. Nonny's salvation is effected through the omnipotence of art as an agent in the revitalization of consciousness, whereas Susanne's final deliverance comes at the hands of a noncreative unesthetic personification of Christian charity. Clemens senses the guilt of others and accepts it as his own. It was precisely this manner of resolution which Karen Blixen reacted so strongly against in her essay on *Rytteren*. She questioned whether the eternally helpful, organizational, and adaptive—but never creative—Clemens was capable of forging Susanne into a whole being.[30] She simply could not accept Clemens as capable of resolving anyone's anxieties and thereby effecting a transformation of the soul. Naturally, one should not demand reality of incident in a myth, but one is entitled to expect reality of effect. Karen Blixen had touched on the central problem in *Rytteren*: the credibility of its resolution which is Susanne's transformation. She makes allowances for a necessarily mythical interpretation by exposing the novel's logical inconsistencies. For example, after Susanne's suicide attempt with sleeping pills in *Evening*, she is immediately responsive to Clemens after a brief interval in *Night*. Thus, in terms of symbolism, incidental order and structure *Rytteren* demands a mythical interpretation, but its resolution may seem unsatisfactory and improbable even when interpreted as myth. Karen Blixen contended that Clemens was ineffective even when viewed as a mythical savior: he helps people without participation from the other person and, so long as he does so, he resolves less than he degrades.[31] He denies the person he helps the pride achieved from the self-determination of one's fate. In the novel's mythical existence there is no possibility of a Platonic identification of the good with the truly real, and Clemens's goodness and charity are merely fictional ideals. They are fictional even to him, for he constantly reproaches himself for his guilt. One striking feature of *Rytteren* in comparison with the later *Söskende* is its total lack of ethical considerations. Justice, an overriding concern in *Söskende*, never appears in *Rytteren*, for ethical considerations can only appear when the truth has been ascertained, and it is the compulsive effort on the part of *Rytteren*'s characters to talk out and seek the truth of who killed Hubert that directs the novel's narrative flow. It is with these evaluations in mind that we now turn to a closer analysis of the novel itself.

In the first scene in "Morning" we meet Susanne alone with Berta, Clemens's housekeeper. Berta resents Susanne's presence, and Susanne is well aware of her resentment. Susanne then reflects on her position in the house and her feeling that she has just come for a brief visit. She doesn't know how or why she came to Clemens. There is no indication of how long she has been living with Clemens, nor when Hubert died. In the play, however, there is a hint at the conclusion of Act II that a year has passed.[32] Berta is a fictive mistress of goodness, while Susanne has become a mistress in fact. As Frederiksen[33] points out, "Morning" is punctuated with the terminology and observational approach of depth psychology. One instance of this is Berta's identification as an angel, which points to Freud's angelism, one's unhealthy psychological identification with high ideals and persons. The contrast between Berta and Susanne is an effective mode of characterization which serves to establish Susanne as an exponent of the same animalistic nature that Hubert represents. Susanne's hair is like a horse's mane and she is well aware of her role as the image of a horse. Susanne combs Berta's hair and comments that it is loose and soft and not like a horse's mane as hers is. Thus compulsive goodness is effectively contrasted with animalism, the image of a centaur, in the novel's initial passages. The scene then shifts to Clemens who is making a house call and then returns home to Susanne. This is the first of two scenes in which Clemens's day breaks through and he is allowed to reflect upon himself and his past while committed to good works. Both scenes are necessarily omitted in the dramatic version. The second aside with Clemens occurs in the third chapter, "Afternoon," after Susanne's encounter with Herman. Clemens is then on a visit to a pregnant woman who has attempted suicide. In the first reflective aside Clemens reviews his conception of God. He had begun by praying to God and ended by praying to himself, to the god within himself. Elsewhere he is referred to as a fat little vain god. Clemens is thereby established as a theophoric image of goodness. He also comments on his vanity and his sense of guilt. He has come to visit an old woman on her deathbed, and he envisions her as his mother, the mother he never knew, for she had died in childbirth. His vision is substantiated by the old woman's physical presence, for she is lying in her bridal nightgown, and he can only conceptualize his mother as innocent of his father's sexual desires. While driving home, he runs into an apple cart. He picks up the apples, pays for the damages and regards himself as an inept clown. Susanne has now been symbolically aligned with Hubert, the centaur, who is not discussed until the conclusion of "Morning," and Clemens has been portrayed with his vanity, clownish ineptitude and burden of self-imposed guilt. In the final scene of this chapter Clemens and Susanne discuss the dead Hubert, and the chapter concludes with Susanne's scream after she has related the nightmare of Hubert's death and recalled his diabolic laughter as he died.

In the following chapter, "Noon," Susanne and Clemens compulsively continue their discussion of Hubert. Clemens relates that he had known Hubert at boarding school, and he tells how he had helped Hubert with his lessons and how he told the school authorities that Hubert had been leaving the school at night to see a girl. Hubert was expelled from the school, and Clemens had then asked him for forgiveness. His role as an informant had provided yet another source of guilt.

In "Afternoon" Susanne leaves Clemens's house—partially at Clemens's request—to set out on her quest for personal identity and affirmation or denial of her view of the past. She first visits Herman who had taken over the riding school after Hubert's death and then Michala who had first met Hubert as a young girl when he had boarded at her father's house. Her father was a clergyman intent on the salvation of problematic boys. Interpolated between these scenes is Clemens's second reflective aside. Herman and Michala are both projections of Hubert's being, as both have been cerebrally forged by him. Hubert had used Herman homosexually, and he had laughed at Michala's advances. She now claims that he had raped her, but in reality she had convinced herself that loving him was the same as loving God and had offered herself to him when a young girl. Both Michala and Herman identified Hubert as a natural deity in life, and both have attempted to reject this identification in death. Both hated him for the restrictive power and control he exerted over their lives. Michala has now become a freedom fanatic, demanding that everyone assert his personal freedom. At the same time she wishes to bind Susanne to her, for she identifies Susanne with Hubert, the same identification Herman makes. As a Lesbian, she desperately needs Susanne whom she now visualizes as a female projection of Hubert. Herman now insists on asserting the discipline he lacked while Hubert was alive, and, similarly, Michala now demands freedom, an unobtainable goal while Hubert was alive. They are both tragically asserting qualities of character voided by Hubert's presence and neutralized within them by his animalistic coercion, a coercion he never consciously exerted, but which was a natural correlative of his being. For both Herman and Michala becoming has now assumed absolute priority over being. Hubert was, as Karen Blixen labels him in her essay, a centaur, and Herman is attempting to replace the dead centaur by reincarnating himself as Hubert.

Susanne's visits to Herman and Michala are instrumental in effecting her psychic transformation: her transition from total dependency on the dead Hubert to the realization of herself as an independent being. In doing so she becomes, as Vosmar points out,[34] an active participant in the process of individuation. The life styles and attitudes of Herman and Michala expose the evils of absolute dependence on Hubert. Herman, who now considers himself the new centaur, attempts to rape Susanne. His life has become a mad vision of discipline and power. Susanne then treats Herman like he treats his horses. She brutally dominates him and presents him with a lump of sugar as if he were a horse. Herman is actually afraid of horses, for he sees the image of the dead Hubert whom he feared reflected in their eyes. Hubert's image is also reflected in Susanne, and he then fears her as he had feared Hubert. To make love to her would be effectually the same as making love to Hubert. Whereas Herman is humiliated and destroyed by acceptance of the lump of sugar, Hubert would have accepted it as a sign of Susanne's love for him. It would have been a physical manifestation of Susanne's emotional recognition of his character. In one symbolic act Susanne has asserted independence of action, an essential step toward individuation and liberation from the specter of the dead Hubert. She must also realize that she can never similarly humiliate Clemens by effecting a symbolic reference to Hubert. Clemens, the person least affected by Hubert's natural coercion, can thereby become the subject of her genuine love, her compulsive tenderness and will to submission. Susanne concludes her visit to Herman with the forceful offering of the

Dramatic Interlude

lump of sugar, and the scene then shifts to Clemens's second aside as he treats the pregnant woman who has attempted suicide. We now see Clemens in his role as the healer. His words to her invalidate any interpretation of Clemens as a Christ figure, for they are mere platitudes, and Christ's parables of virtue can hardly be translated as platitudes. He actually degrades the poor woman by holding out fantastic promises, and then he reproaches himself for being a vain clown and he feels guilty for his ineptitude as an agent of salvation. His goodness has its origin in weakness and is activated by his guilty conscience. Clemens's character is described by the multiplicity of glosses for *skyld,* which incorporates the semantic fields covered by "fault, blame, debt, transgression, trespasses and sake." His goodness is motivated by guilt, and his sensation of guilt is engendered by his feeling of ineptitude in the accomplishment of good works. Therefore, Clemens's nature is necessarily cyclical. He has a perpetual sense of *déjà vu,* of circumstantial repetition. The emotional translation of guilt is fright, and fright obstructs the apprehension of God, if God is viewed as a domineering father figure. Clemens has never used the word God. In the concluding chapter, "Night," Susanne asks Clemens if he believes in God, and he answers: "I don't know what it is. I know no other word for it than humanity." [35] *Rytteren* is not, as Vosmar suggests,[36] the first instance of Branner's use of the Freudian doctrine that the concept of God is a father figure. As we have seen, this view was introduced in *Historien om Börge.* Clemens's relation to his father is practically the same as Börge's. It is a relation of corporal distance and awe, as we note in "Noon":

"I come from a Christian home," he said. "I grew up with original sin. And even if my father did not accuse me directly . . ."
"Accuse you!"
"I just said that he didn't accuse me. But he treated me differently from my brothers and sisters. It seems to me that he never spoke directly to me, only through them." [37]

A few pages later in the same chapter Clemens's restrictive concern with goodness, guilt and orginal sin is symbolically contrasted with Hubert's complete lack of concern for these concepts:

The ritual again, Clemens thought wearily. The analyst behind his screen. The father confessor in his chair. The eternally same questions and answers. Back, back to childhood. Back to original sin. Back to the time before sin, a time when horses wandered freely over misty plains.[38]

While Clemens is satisfied with the mere contemplation of childhood as a period of innocence, Michala actually wants to revert to childhood, to become an innocent child again and thereby free of guilt. With the conclusion of Clemens's second aside, the scene then shifts to Susanne's visit to Michala. Michala wants to give Susanne a picture of a man on horseback as a birthday present. The picture was painted by a seven-year-old child, and Michala asserts that it represents a child's view of freedom and that freedom is nothing more than a child. She wears an amulet of a child around her neck. Michala wants to return to childhood as a period before sin, a period when her life had not yet been altered by Hubert. When she finally confesses the truth behind her lie that Hubert had attempted to rape her, then she is destroyed as an individual in Susanne's eyes, and Susanne sees her as a child. Having exorcised her lie of life, she has ceased to exist as a vital being.

Whereas the image of the horse dominates the first three chapters, the human image dominates the two final chapters, and the shift in the novel's mental climate is indicated by its shift in symbolic values. In "Evening" Susanne returns to Clemens, who has been waiting for her to celebrate her birthday, and her psychic rebirth is now about to enter its concluding phase. Susanne compulsively relates the scene of Hubert's death once more. Clemens then emphatically states that it was she who killed Hubert. Their relationship had been purely sensual. Susanne had made sex her total and pitiable shield against an awareness of life and had viewed sex as an iterative death. At the conclusion of "Evening" Clemens leaves to rescue the pregnant woman from her suicide attempt, the one woman of whom he has demanded a suicide attempt, after he has prepared everything for Susanne's attempt at suicide—and salvation.[39] After Clemens leaves, Susanne attempts suicide, and she is revived when Clemens returns in "Night." She is prevented from choosing death as a way of saving her freedom, but she is still confronted by death—by a change of personality so complete that she cannot survive as the person she is. Clemens then again accuses Susanne of having killed

Dramatic Interlude

Hubert. She then relates Hubert's last words, a detail of the death scene she had never told before. Throughout the novel Hubert has been portrayed as taciturn. We are repeatedly told that he rarely spoke. As an animalistic image, verbal communication was not a part of his character. Hubert's last words come forth as they might resound from the splendid silence of a Greek tragedy. When Susanne had approached the dying Hubert with a cup of water, he had refused it and said: "I don't know you. Go away. I want Clemens—Clemens." These words finally explain why Susanne had come to Clemens. Clemens has grown in power and stature throughout the course of the novel. He has exerted influence and control over the lives of those about him and with Susanne's restatement of Hubert's final words, we realize that Clemens has become the new centaur, the new center of mortal force with mythic proportions. His control over the lives of the others is even clearer in the dramatic version of *Rytteren*. In the novel only two characters are ever on the stage at once. In the play, however, Michala comes to visit Susanne and Clemens, and Clemens's power over her is distinct and decisive. His suggestion that Susanne visit Herman in the novel is practically a command in the play. Then, too, the critical relationship between goodness and the necessity for guilt is succinctly clarified in the play. In both versions Susanne says that she believes Clemens is responsible for everybody's death, but that he has given her her life. In the novel Clemens replies:

"Be quiet," he said. "It was my fault. Solely my fault. I shouldn't have said that." [40]

but in the play he says:

CLEMENS (tearing himself loose): Above all I wanted to be guilty for yours. That's why I'm reproaching myself. —I shouldn't have said that, Susanne.[41]

In the novel we have an insistence on assuming the sole responsibility for Susanne's suicide attempt, but in the play we have a statement of desire and causation. It is as if Clemens wanted to have Susanne succeed in her attempt, so that he would have a maximal source for his guilt anxiety, so that he would achieve a burden of guilt so large that he would be perpetually driven to perform good works as acts of contrition. When Susanne then repeats Hubert's last words, then Clemens necessarily achieves an enormity of guilt anxiety for ever having permitted her attempt: Hubert has seen Clemens as his salvation and therefore also as Susanne's. Thus Clemens was required to effect Susanne's spiritual transformation. His near failure as the agent of Susanne's transformation has been caused by the cyclical nature of his psychic responses, and therefore his portrayal as a character is both internally consistent and ultimately credible.

In *Rytteren* myth and mystery are spliced together as legend, and the novel surely ranks as one of the towering accomplishments of contemporary Danish prose. It incorporates many of Branner's favorite motifs and images. It is overladen with hand symbolism.[42] The pregnant woman has the small brown hands of Merete Rude, and we recall that the doctor in *Drömmen om en Kvinde* is also named Clemens. Susanne is obsessed with Clemens's hands. She strokes Michala's head with her hands and defiantly thinks they are Clemens's hands. Offstage dying, first employed in *Eftermæle,* is reintroduced here. There is the identification of God as a father figure which we find again in *Söskende*. Then, too, as Vosmar has indicated,[43] Hubert is reminiscent of Hans Egge in *Barnet leger ved Stranden*. Both are exponents of supernatural powers who stand behind the enfolding action and never appear, yet they control the lives of those on stage. Both have been instrumental in forming the woman who is dramatically central in the linear progression of a plot. The rhythmic pattern of *Rytteren* is punctuated by waking and sleeping. Susanne awakens on the morning of her thirty-second birthday to a new psychic life. She attempts to kill herself with sleep, and then awakens to her final transformation. This pattern is employed again in *Ingen kender Natten.*

In an interview conducted three years after *Rytteren* had appeared,[44] Branner contended that the novel had been interpreted to death and that the critics had once again discovered symbols never intentionally inserted. Any analysis of *Rytteren* poses the dangerous temptation of a symbol hunt, but this is necessarily due to its panoramic vision and almost inexhaustible wealth of images. On New Year's Day a year after its appearance Branner published a short story entitled, *Samtale med en Klovn*,[45] which is his poetic answer to the storm of criticism that greeted *Rytteren*.

Early one January morning an author leaves his house for a walk. Thinking he is completely alone, he is surprised when he meets a clown whom he feels he has known "for months and years." The clown is Clemens's *Doppelgänger* and the author's *alter ego*, the physical manifestation of Clemens's clownish ineptitude. The author, too, is realized as both aggressive and clownish and laughs at his fear of the dark. After a few introductory remarks on the stormy weather, the clown suddenly remarks that it is difficult to love reality and not to flee from it. The author replies that he has listened to the clown's transcendental nonsense long enough. He regards the clown as a figure he has often used in his game as an author. If, as the clown says, the author loves the dark and the storm, then it is only because, as the author says, he has used them as symbols for hate and doubt. He loves both, as they are dramatic essentials. Shortly thereafter the clown performs a miracle at the author's request and calms the storm as Christ had done. The critical assumption that Clemens was intended as a Christ figure is here being subjected to sublime ridicule. The clown then states that black magic is cheap, for it teaches nothing about reality, and he then embarks on a philosophical discussion. Many of the clown's responses are contextually the same as Clemens's words to Susanne. We have freedom only to love. Power is nothing other than a word for fear. He who loves is free of fear. The poet finally becomes furious with the clown, the clown within him, and grabs him, shaking him until he begs for mercy. The storm blows up again, and the clown says that he is the poet, but the poet can never be him. The clown then attempts to express the unutterable in a dance. Philosophical speculation has been translated into physical sensation, and the clown in his dance cries out to the crucified Christ as his clothes are ripped away in the storm and his limbs become dancing flames.

As we have seen, Clemens was definitely not a positively good man, and *Samtale med en Klovn* as a poetic response to *Rytteren's* critics reaffirms our assertion that Branner never intended Clemens to represent the idea of absolute goodness. The Christ figure is a clown in this world and is consumed by its own miraculous lack of reality. Perfect goodness in the actuality of this world has a place as an ideal only or in the realm of religious metaphysics. Branner's clown is Ibsen's troll.

Samtale med en Klovn occupies an important position in Branner's production, for it offers insight into his desire to temporarily renounce the fantastic and mythical with a return to realism. In *Rytteren* he had achieved a unification of the comic with the pathetic to expose the area wherein religious intensity often hides itself in the modern world, although these same attributes had been the most respected manifestations of religiosity in earlier periods of man's intellectual endeavor. It is one of the most demanding exercises in modern literature to place myth in a contemporary setting, something Karen Blixen was to do on only one occasion, namely in *Spögelseshestene,* fittingly enough her response to *Rytteren*. With the conclusion of *Rytteren* Branner was to turn to naturalistic drama in *Söskende,* and he stated that he had intentionally chosen a more realistic form than in *Rytteren*.[46]

Söskende[47] is a three act drama set in an Ibsenesque drawing room. It is far more in the naturalistic vein than in the experimental tradition of, let us say, the Moscow Art Theater or the expressionistic avant-garde of Jacques Copeau or Jean Cocteau. In *Söskende* Judge Olden, although he is never seen, is the dominating figure. He plays essentially the same role in this play as Hubert plays in *Rytteren*. He is discussed, feared, hated and respected. Olden has shaped and controlled the lives of his children, Arthur, Irene and Michael. In the opening scene we hear Olden crying like a baby in the bedroom upstairs, but his cries alternate with animalistic roars. He alternates between overpowering, raging strength and infantile weakness. He makes his desires and feelings known by tapping on the floor overhead with a walking stick. We feel his presence in precisely the same way as we feel John Gabriel Borkman's presence in the Ibsen play. His portrait has the same central position on stage as does the portrait of Hedda Gabler's father. His writing desk, too, is given a central position on stage, and it is probably there that his legal opinions were composed. Judge Olden symbolizes the law of the Old Testament, and his walking staff is the staff of righteousness, the prop of the indisputable prophet of a stern and incontrovertible God. Although Judge Olden was called "the silent one" by the villagers, he has now become a raging monster on his deathbed. He bit his

Dramatic Interlude

nurse, Sister Agnes. He cannot bear to have his children near him, as he cannot bear to see how his judgments have affected their lives, and his judicious aloofness seems to have driven him mad. He now has an ambiguous physical position in the world he has judged. Sister Agnes says that it is uncertain whether or not he is eventually going to live or die, or he may linger on in the half-life of a coma. Thus, while his children are assembled in the drawing room below, he may still be passing judgment on them, or he may give up his case and die, or he may withhold judgment while in a coma.

Olden's three children have also passed judgment on the way he has raised them. They have done so in the way they have reacted to life. Arthur, like Clemens in *Rytteren,* has tried to live his life as a paragon of virtue and other directed goodness. He has tried to become as successful an attorney as his father was and, like him, to become a judge. Like Clemens, too, he has tried to help people by interpreting the laws governing mankind. In short, Arthur has attempted to carry out the self-imposed duty of complying with his interpretation of what his father judged that he should do. Michael is diametrically opposed to Arthur. Just as Arthur has followed the path of duty, Michael has always wanted complete freedom from any obligation. Arthur has completely denied himself in order to obtain a self-imposed goal, whereas Michael's only goal was self-fulfillment. The brothers represent the extremes of two essentially ethical choices, though the point of departure for both has been the same: a reaction to their father's judgment. Michael has attempted to reject all laws, while Arthur has attempted to comply with all of his father's legal precepts. Nevertheless, neither of the brothers has achieved his objective, and Olden is the image which blocks both sons on their diametrically opposed roads to self-fulfillment. He is the specter which haunts the minds of those about him, a specter of which they must absolve themselves if they are to achieve individuation. Olden has thwarted his sons in their personal quests, as he wanted them to fulfill him and not themselves. In this, also, he is very like Hubert in *Rytteren.* Arthur, the good boy, has denied himself in attempting to fulfill his father; he has never made love, has never allowed himself to consider freedom as an objective and has bound himself to the absolute of restrictive duty. On the other hand, Michael, the adventurous, has sought freedom in vain.

Arthur has been overwhelmed by the responsibility of the law, while Michael has devoted all his psychic energies to a total rejection of the law in all of its prescriptive aspects. Both represent absolutes: absolute freedom from and absolute obedience to prescriptive laws. Within the terms of these absolutes each has conducted a search for personal happiness. In shaping their attitudes toward prescriptive laws, Judge Olden has shaped their personalities, and the basis for the conflict between them is the natural antagonism between their personal motives.

The setting of an Ibsenesque drawing room is admirably suited for the debate which ensues between the two brothers. Their debate forms the outer action of the play, and their sister Irene is the mediator of that debate. The play's inner action is conducted on both a spiritual and a psychological level. The latter is indicated symbolically by the cathartic quality of Irene's mediatory grace. Symbolically, Olden represents the divine law in whom all authority is vested. His unseen presence sets the spiritual tone of the play, and he may be regarded as an unseen and dying god, an Old Testament Jehova easily moved to wrath.

Michael is the most problematic figure in the play, and his presence creates its central dramatic tension. He sees himself both as a Christ figure and as his namesake, the archangel Michael. To support this self-indulgent fantasy, he has become a compulsive liar. For example, he says that he once helped a woman commit suicide, and Irene then takes up her role as mediator by asking:

IRENE: Are you telling the truth, Michael?
MICHAEL: As I see it, yes.
IRENE: Ah, but should we all see it so? Is it really the truth?
MICHAEL: What is the truth except that we each of us choose to believe—every man for himself? [48]

and Arthur then interrupts as a legal prosecutor:

ARTHUR: Irene! (to Michael) We will stop talking in riddles please. Will you kindly answer one or two questions? [49]

Irene is a mediator between two views of the truth: the fantastic and disjunctive vs. the realistic and conjunctive. Arthur represents the views of his father, the views of the Old Testament

Dramatic Interlude

Jehova, while Michael, who is symbolically sketched as a Christ-figure, represents the modified views of the New Testament which are to be reconciled with those of the Old. At first this interpretation may sound as if we are reading too much symbolic meaning into the play, but it can easily be demonstrated that the play is actually overladen with symbolism. After *Rytteren*'s reception by some critics as a cloudy, somewhat misunderstood work, Branner may have felt it imperative to make *Søskende* as lucid as possible. The unifying symbol of the whole design is made conceptually visible by a strong dependence on the readily recognizable attributes of Christian mythology. The characters are provided with the clear outlines of conventional Biblical masks. Theme and recognition are symbolized by the emblematic objects of Christianity. The structural conditions of movement and order are organized by reference to the natural cycle which finds its expression in the mythical figure of Olden, the dying god, who represents that cycle. Michael is clearly drawn as a Christ figure. When Sister Agnes first sees the tattered Michael, she places him beside the fire and goes to fetch him the Judge's slippers. As Michael is sitting in his father's chair before the fire, the arm comes off and he holds it up as a scepter while he waits for Irene to wash his bloody feet. As a self-enthroned Christian prince, Michael proceeds to tell about his adventures during the war. After his ship had been torpedoed, he floundered about in the sea and finally succeeded in climbing aboard a raft of floating timbers. He lay there stretched out on his back for several days while the gulls picked at him. Michael had been crucified by the freedom he sought:

MICHAEL: And now I am both Father and Son. I am Judge and Judged. I have hanged myself upon a cross. [———] Take me down, Sister. —Take me down if you can—.[50]

Michael has undergone a *pietà*, but with one important exception: there has been no miracle of love. In his mind Michael's search for freedom has taken the form of a passion play of unbelievable horror and suffering. For him, freedom has been a negative value, for it has led to estrangement and alienation from all human fellowship. Like Susanne before her spiritual metamorphosis, Michael is a product of anxiety rooted in loneliness. Thus, at the end of Act One, a dying god is judging his children and damning them in absentia. A miracle of love must occur in the temple of order and justice before this condemnatory judgment can be nullified.

As Irene is the mediator of the Arthur vs. Michael debate and therefore structurally pivotal, then it might be expected that, if any miracle of love is to occur, then she will be its agent. Irene is married to Adam, a war profiteer just like Gabriel Blom in *Ingen kender Natten* and Henry in *Thermopylæ*. In terms of sexual experience Irene stands midway between her brothers: she has loved only Adam, Arthur is a virgin, and Michael has slept with scores of women.

The debate in Act Two takes the form of a Platonic symposium on spiritual love which concludes harmoniously, whereupon Olden's death is announced. In the beginning of the act, Irene defended her father on realistic grounds, for she demythologized him, as she sees him for what he is: a senile old man who does not know what he is doing. Having heard her defense, Michael stages a violent outburst directed at the source of his frustration: his father. Like Clemens in *Rytteren,* he accuses his father for having caused his mother's death. He hates his father, but he has not, like Clemens, learned to overcome his hatred. He says that his father killed his mother by denying her love. Arthur is vainly searching for a motive to support his father rejection, and his attitude toward him is clearly schizoid. He rejects him for imaginative crimes against his mother, while he simultaneously admires him and fears him for his judicious vision. Irene then continues to defend her father, and she is joined in her attempt by Arthur. She attempts to make Arthur see the Judge, not as an idol to be worshiped, but with a judicious eye as a human being. Unlike both Arthur and Michael, Irene has benefited from Olden's teachings, for she has become a careful and just judge of humanity. She has actively replaced her father as judge and mediator. Irene attempts to prove that Olden actually loved Michael, because Michael was most like his mother, whom Olden had actually loved but for whom he could not express his love. Like Arthur, Olden felt that to judge people impartially he had to beware of becoming too emotionally involved with them. He pressed the concept of absolute justice so far that he became frozen off from the human context of that concept. Olden represents the tragic fallacy of the

Dramatic Interlude 117

active humanist. Although he had accepted the responsibility of aiding others, he was incapable of the love necessary to effect that responsibility. Consequently, his humanism suffered a spiritual paralysis, symbolized by his physical condition during the first two acts.

Through her persuasive efforts Irene gradually begins to make Michael and Arthur aware of what Olden actually represents. She has demythologized the source of their personal anxieties. Once that source has been reduced to rational terms, then both Arthur and Michael gain the insight necessary to resolve their anxieties; both men begin to recognize themselves for what they are and to accept themselves with all their defects. Michael then tells Arthur that, for all his lifelessness, he was the only dependable person in a lawless world. Michael confesses that the freedom he achieved was in fact a living hell. Both brothers then turn to Irene and question her about her life and whether or not she has found the happiness which has eluded them. Irene confesses that she is terribly unhappy with Adam and that he is in love with another woman. She also tells them that she has taken a young lover—the man who drove her to Olden's. The confession is slow and painful:

IRENE: Love is such a hard word. One can't really use it. But I would like to help him—only I can't. It is like sitting with a crying child on one's knee and not knowing how to comfort it—because it can't understand one's words. (She sits down.) You mustn't think—I haven't ever talked about him like this before. And one lies to oneself too. Besides, he was a wonderful lover once. Before he got rich. I can't forget that.[51]

Here, as in many of Pär Lagerkvist's plays, the unsaid is just as important as the said. Indication of the unsaid, which is disclosed by Irene's pauses, creates an atmosphere of the mind and permits the viewer to glimpse the deepest recesses of the speaker's psyche. Irene has now opened up her mind to her brothers, drawn them into her confidence, and asked them to console her just as they have been consoled by her. Following her confession, Michael states that he has slept with so many women that he has actually slept with none, for he cannot clearly distinguish any one woman from all those he has had. Irene then describes him as a lover:

IRENE: You are no different from the men where I come from—
the land of might and money. You are all fighters with blood on your
hands. Hate and fear—that is what you have to offer a woman. That
is what you force us to accept.[52]

With Arthur's final confession that he is a virgin, the three have
confessed the results of their quests for sexual happiness. Their
motivations have differed, but their quests have all led to negative
results. Arthur has loved his father and rejected him, and he has
become frustrated for not having received any recognition or respect for his limited judicial talents. Michael, like Hubert in *Rytteren,* merely sought to dominate women, and he has received no
love in return. Irene has attempted to help her husband by giving
him love, but she has been completely thwarted in her efforts.
Having recognized and confessed their flaws to each other, they
can now be bound together by mutual love. Irene stands between
her brothers and grasps their hands. They will live together and
build a dream cottage. Michael will cease wandering, and Arthur
will give up the law and become a gardener, while Irene will take
care of the cottage. The light above the Judge's portrait grows
dim, but at the same time a burst of light enters the room and
exposes its shabbiness. A flute playing a nursery tune is heard in
the background, and the three siblings are transported to a land of
childish innocence. Agnes then enters the room to announce that
the Judge is dead. The curtain falls on Act Two.

The miracle of love is dispelled forever in the final act. The
room grows dark once more, and the illusion of peaceful harmony
is broken when the undertaker coldly relates the practical details
for the funeral. Arthur, Irene and Michael begin to realize once
more the power which their father has had over them. Arthur
begins to reassess his father, and concludes that Olden represented
absolute justice outside the necessary limits of human relations.
Michael soon realizes that the dream of the bucolic life is being
destroyed. Irene persists in her view that Olden was nothing more
nor less than a lonely old man desirous of human affection. When
Agnes reenters the room, Michael asks her how old she is, and it is
obvious that he has sighted yet another victim for his flesh mill.
He then takes a seven-branched candlestick and approaches his
father's portrait as if he were to make a votive offering. Symbolically, he is a prophet approaching a portrait of the Old Testament

Dramatic Interlude

Jehova while holding aloft the lights of the seven original cities of Christendom. Michael has reverted to his earlier role as a Christ figure. Arthur then discovers that he has been appointed a public prosecutor and departs for Copenhagen to continue along the path of duty. Irene has clearly failed in her attempt to perform a miracle of love and transformation. She is aware of her failure, but dismisses it:

> IRENE: Only a self-murderer. Rise above it or go under—no one can help you. I have nothing more to say. (*She stands at the door in her coat ready to go, but turns toward him again.*) Oh, dear Michael, I am your sister—I love you. But I simply had to say something. The age of miracles is over. We have to perform them ourselves now.[53]

Irene departs and Michael is left alone with Agnes, who, like Berta in *Rytteren*, represents Christian charity. He wants her to say the Lord's Prayer with him. He has set himself up as the Anti-Christ and attempts to seduce Agnes, only to discover that she has no conception of wickedness and actually loves him. Finally, having said that he will go to sea again, he leaves, and the curtain falls on the final act.

The play ends as it began; the wheel of tragedy has come full circle. Three siblings have met together, renounced their disparate quests after having recognized their futility, attempted to find happiness together, and departed from each other with the same quests in mind as when they first came into Olden's study. They have all tried to find absolute happiness through absolute goals. Both Arthur and Michael have tried to emulate their father, but the ways in which they have chosen to do so are diametrically opposed. Arthur has clung to the absolute authority of the law which he thought his father represented, while Michael has named himself an absolute authority. It is Michael who has most nearly succeeded in imitating his father, for Michael has established himself as an absolute judge. Of course, he is a false imitation, for the judgments he makes are the inverse of those his father made.

Söskende was received with many of the same critical objections as *Rytteren*. Its structure was thought to be too contrived, too schematic, and it was prematurely dismissed as lacking in dramatic power. Stephan Hurwitz,[54] a professor of jurisprudence, questioned its apparent lack of psychological motivation, as well as its unrealistic portrayal of the judge as a symbol of absolute justice. He concluded that Branner had mistakenly oversimplified the concept of justice by defining it as unequivocally nonrelative. Nevertheless, despite such objections, the passage of time has proven *Söskende* a successful stage play and established Branner as a forceful and resourceful contributor to contemporary Danish theater; it has enjoyed many successful performances both in Denmark and abroad. Moreover, it is fitting that we should depart from a strictly chronological consideration of Branner's works in discussing *Söskende* and *Rytteren* together, for thematically they may be viewed as components of a cycle. In its portrayal of Hubert as a natural force unencumbered by tradition, *Rytteren* is the myth of the rising god before the Fall, while *Söskende* contains the myth of the dying god whose legalistic prescriptions for good and evil have been invalidated by experience.

Judge Olden's last words were a plea to see Michael, and here we are reminded of the dying Hubert's plea to see Clemens: both men finally desire contact with those characters who superficially represent direct antitheses to their own characters. However, on closer inspection, we may question the implication of antithesis in these relationships. Hubert represents the very life force of nature devoid of communal responsibility, while Clemens is reason and sensitivity apart from the elemental power of erotic nature. Olden is the acerbic judge, while Michael seems to lack self-judgment in his conviction that he is the Anti-Christ. In the last moment of his life Hubert demanded the presence of the only other person who had accepted full responsibility for his actions, no matter how diametrically opposed to his own those actions might have been. In the same manner, Olden wants to see Michael, the only other person in the drama who accepts full responsibility for his actions. These are the dimensions of the affinities between these characters. Hubert and Olden are representatives of *a priori* mythical order. Hubert existed in a natural order before the Fall, and Olden is the Old Testament patriarch, a dying god, confronted with the Anti-Christ. Then, too, there is a spiritual affinity between Michael and Clemens. Michael lacks Clemens's sense of social responsibility. Both are possessed of the undimensionality of personal faith and spiritual loneliness. Michael had, as Vosmar points out,[55] drained the cup of human suffering while on the raft and had thereby symbolically taken part in Christ's death. There-

Dramatic Interlude

fore, he can never return to conventional reality. He is necessarily conditioned by a mystical, visionary view of life, just as Clemens, Hubert and Olden are so conditioned. All four are capable of psychic transformation and can exist as free beings within the confines of self-determined responsibilities. Hubert is responsible to the laws of nature, Olden to absolute justice, Clemens to charity and Michael to nihilism expressed as the blasphemy of the Anti-Christ.[56] All four are representations of the self in anticipation of its absolute calling and destiny.

In terms of themes, formal properties, and characters, *Rytteren* and *Söskende* are clearly related, and the latter stands as a response to the unanswered questions of the former. The unifying theme of both is the transformational power of love confronted with the unresolvable contradictions of personal freedom. Whereas the conclusion of *Rytteren* reaffirms the transformational power of love, *Söskende* is one of Branner's darkest works and concludes as a denial of love's transformational power. In *Söskende* the miracle of love never occurs, and hope is humiliated and frustrated by the contradictions within the human soul. The ethical meaning of various human projects has been defined against the background of a specter of absolute justice. However, the absolutist view of life is condemned to failure in both works, as is symbolized by the deaths of Hubert and Olden, the respective representatives of absolute freedom and justice. The question of whether or not man can achieve love and responsibility is finally answered in *Söskende* with an almost desperate pessimism.

With the conclusion of *Söskende* Branner entered upon one of the darkest periods in his creative life. The vision of hope extended in the earlier works had vanished in lieu of a positive interpretation of human values. That vision was not to recur again until the conclusion of *Ingen kender Natten,* which marks the initiation of a new phase in his career, a phase in which he was to reaffirm his message that one can only bind oneself to life if one accepts the responsibility of social action. In *Rytteren* and *Söskende,* however, Branner had distinguished himself as a teller of tales of mythical proportions far removed from the stark realism of the 1930s as reflected in *Legetöj* and his early short stories. Now he was to turn inward upon himself in a series of deeply personal works in a search for the creative images which forged *Ingen kender Natten* into one of his finest achievements.

CHAPTER 5

The End of a Phase and Ingen kender Natten

BJERGENE,[1] said to have been written in 1946 and 1951, has at least a thematic relationship with *Trommerne* and *Angst*, though there are a multitude of differences between *Bjergene* on the one hand and *Trommerne* and *Angst* on the other. *Bjergene*, like the earlier stories, tells of an author in search of himself:

—I've come to closing my eyes and opening them again—and in the meantime the dream has become reality, but the reality has become a dream without meaning.[2]

The author in *Bjergene*, unlike the author in *Angst* and *Trommerne*, is not the narrator. More important, he is named, and has not, therefore, completely lost his identity. Then, too, the author in *Bjergene* has a wife who is not only named, but who also takes an active part in the story. In *Bjergene*, as opposed to *Angst* and *Trommerne*, the war has ended and the author, Claus, and his wife, Winnie, who are both middle-aged, have returned to Germany to stay in a hotel along the Bodensee. Despite these differences, *Angst*, *Trommerne*, and *Bjergene* are similar in that all three are Ingmar Bergman-like attempts to exteriorize an artist's mortal combat with the demons of his own obsessions, compulsions and self-contempt.

The author in *Bjergene* is well known and widely respected. He has arrived, but upon arrival he believes that his creative powers have begun to weaken and that his sensitivity and feeling for words have been greatly diminished. All has become a meaningless dream. He has lost contact with reality and strips himself bare as a poet attempting to regain his creative power and consciousness through regaining contact with his wife. In a scene which is strongly reminiscent of the dying Mortimer in *Drömmen om en*

The End of a Phase and Ingen kender Natten

Kvinde, Claus, too, tries to regenerate contact with life by regenerating contact with his wife:

"I don't know what there is that is myself. I don't know what truth is." He looked down at the play of the two hands. "No, that's not the truth," he said. "Keep it up," he said. For perhaps, if she continued to stroke his palm with her finger tips, then perhaps he could realize that source again and laugh again. "Keep it up," he said.[3]

Claus's attempts at spiritual regeneration are doomed to failure. He has become a formless entity adrift in a world in which he knows only boredom and indifference. Different varieties of food and wine taste the same. Faces look alike, words sound alike, and the world about him has become meaningless, for he has lost the power to differentiate, to distinguish between the varied and varying aspects of reality. His indifference has caused him to lose sight of the mountains. In *Bjergene* the mountains, which symbolized an unobtainable love fantasy in *Sidst i August*, are now meant, as Jörn Vosmar suggests,[4] to stand for life, or the truth about life and reality.

In *Bjergene* life is divided into imagined versus lived experiences, and the two are held together by the same splicing technique which was to be used later in *Ingen kender Natten* (1955). The "lived" experiences are those of Claus and Winnie at the hotel on the Bodensee, while the imagined experiences are those of the flashbacks in which Claus observes the disgusting sights of an immediate postwar Germany. The dichotomy between the two lives is spliced together so that the conclusion of one becomes the beginning of another, and an illusion of simultaneity is thereby upheld:

He smiled at his sense of complete security and didn't feel the slightest amazement that he was no longer in his room far beneath the ruins, but in reality—

—in reality he lay with his head in her lap and was encircled by her knees and touched her breast.[5]

There are distinct differences between the Claus of 1946 and the Claus who has come to the hotel along the Bodensee with his wife. The former reacts with sensitivity and feeling to the sights of a destroyed country and its wretched inhabitants, while the latter suffers from emotional paralysis. The former Claus has, as Emil Frederiksen suggests, "absorbed the ruined country's hunger and disease in himself," [6] and the disease erupts in the latter in the form of an attempted suicide. However, both Clauses have attempted to see the inner form of life behind the façade of the mountains, the mountains which symbolize a physical manifestation of the barriers of hate, fear, and cruelty:

> When one saw them from afar they were as innocent as the wings of angels, or as troops of white pilgrims wandering toward the incomprehensible distance, toward death and resurrection, and Lord God Himself, but they were quickly transformed and became hideous and grotesque like gigantic lizards—they slept with one eye half-open and feigned death, but he had heard them roar. He had clung to the outermost link on a serrated dragon's tail and whipped the world into white scum about himself until up and down, far and near became one and the same. No one should say that he didn't know the mountains. He was at home in their temples and holes and grottoes. He had lain prostrate on the holy stone where humans were offered to gods. He had stood under a rainbow of glistening quartz and felt the nearness of the gods: here they had reigned in their demented power and magic, and it was from here that they still mastered the world through demented old men who sucked the blood from people's dreams and selected eagles and beasts as symbols and built abodes beyond all human measure.[7]

Claus on the Bodensee is reflecting on the meaning of the mountains in a passage which, with its run-on of imagery and jumble of symbols, might well have been taken from *Also sprach Zarathustra*. A world vision of white piety can suddenly change itself into something hideous and grotesque with mad gods to suck the life blood from human dreams. The Claus of 1946 has come as a sort of Mosaic prophet to view a paradise from the mount, but, in reality, that paradise is a plain of buildings ground to dust whose inhabitants grovel for cigarettes. The Claus of 1946 is the author of *Döden varer saa længe* (1947)[8] who came to postwar Germany to lecture on *Die Krise des Humanismus* and felt revulsion and disgust at the sound of his own words. The later Claus has attempted to see behind his words, to see reality, and to regain faith in himself as an author. These are the three major demands of *Trommerne*, *Angst*, and *Bjergene*. In *Bjergene* they are couched in the language of an almost incommunicable mystical experience, the experience symbolized by the mountains.

Claus in *Bjergene* might also be said to be the author-narrator in *Digteren og Pigen*[9] who "wanted to write a book, but before he dared begin on it, he had to find a meaning with what happened, both outside him and inside him . . ."[10] Claus must see behind the mountains, and to see behind them is to conduct a search for the meaning of truth and reality:

> He believed that there was one truth, but there were many. He had believed it was fixed and immutable, but it was fleeting like a mirage. He believed it was white or black, but that was the one thing it wasn't. It glistened like a rainbow.[11]

Just as his namesake, Claus in *Barnet leger ved Stranden*, he has attempted to view truth as an absolute and to interpret life in terms of absolutes. His failure to do so has resulted in a mental crisis. Claus has, philosophically speaking, discovered that objective idealism, which implies that things have no reality except such as they have in relation to themselves, is false. He resorts to a mystical interpretation of a world of nature and created spirit, which, by enabling him to exercise his creative energies and redemptive love, also enables him to know and be himself.

The starting point of Claus's philosophy of existence is, as for Kierkegaard, personal anxiety, personal dread. Claus begins in the situation of the Kierkegaardian "absolute paradox" and ends by attempting to make a leap of faith, though Claus's leap takes the form of an attempted suicide.[12] This may be interpreted to imply that to lose one's life is but to gain it, which is precisely what Tomas was to learn in *Ingen kender Natten*.

Though the situation and the cerebral framework of *Bjergene* may be regarded as Kierkegaardian and though taking this view would seem to clarify some of the aspects of the story, we must not impose a rigidly Kierkegaardian interpretation on *Bjergene*. Branner confessed to having been interested in crises of faith, such as we find in *Fear and Trembling*, but he considered Kierkegaard impossible reading and stated that his philosophy had no influence on his writing.[13] Branner is here suggesting that, for Claus, and probably for himself as well,[14] the harsh realities of a Germany destroyed by war contradicted his faith in the ultimate good of man.

Earlier, Claus had sought an absolutely rational interpretation of reality, but the horrors unleashed by the war made such an interpretation impossible. Words no longer had any power to express either a rational or a mystical interpretation of all that he had seen, and reason could only comprehend that reality as insane chaos. In 1946 Claus had reacted sensitively to the sights he saw, but they were so emotionally overpowering that they completely sapped all his sensitivity. The world about him had, in fact, become the very world which Kafka presented in *The Trial* and *The Castle*.[15] The apprehension of reality had become as for Kafka, "a mood of total impotence, of paralysis in the face of the unintelligible power of circumstances."[16] Claus on the Bodensee feels that his power to use words is no longer equal to the emotional presuppositions of their expressive power. Having realized the unutterability of outward reality, he is faced with a paralysis of expressiveness, and all human activity has, consequently, been robbed of meaning and rendered impotent. In this he forms a direct contrast to the author-narrators of *Trommerne* and *Angst* who felt that words and the sensitive use of words were the only weapons left to awaken their fellow men to the demands of communal responsibility. Then, too, the author-narrators of these earlier tales had had a serious intent, while Claus "has always merely lived a game, even on the extreme limits."[17]

No matter whether Claus's interpretation of the world is realistic or mystical, he is still faced with the demands of accepting responsibility and developing a personal faith. Regardless of the interpretive pattern Claus attempts to impose upon reality, there remains but one route open to an apprehension of the truth, and that is the acceptance of these demands. Once, long ago, Claus had said: "God is in me, and I am God,"[18] which recalls the phrase, recurrent in Branner's love scenes: "You are in me, and I am in you." For Claus, the mystical experience of love has been replaced by a mystical experience of the world about him. He has repeatedly attempted to see behind things, behind the mountains, and to pass through the eye of the needle of faith:

I have stood on the top of black, vertical cliffs until I become dizzy and everything floats before my eyes, and I heard the song from the abyss and knew that now, now I must jump. But I didn't jump. I remained standing on the spot and forced my eyes to look down, down the whole time until I saw that the abyss was nothing, and God and the devil were nothing, and it remained up to me whether I would live or die—then for the first time I stepped back a pace from the edge, and since then I haven't had vertigo.[19]

Claus has withstood a test of conviction and will and, in the words of the preface of the 1953 edition of *Bjergene,* he has reached "an outpost whence no route leads further forward." In *Bjergene* Branner has attempted to show that, once on the very brink of despair, man is also on the brink of faith, on the brink of discovering the truth about life, art, and reality; but he dare not step further lest he plunge into the abyss of the unknown. Claus has reached a point where concomitant apprehension of reality and a dissolution of personality have forced him either to accept personal faith and responsibility or to lose his life. That he does not take the final leap into nothingness shows that he has absolved himself of the anxiety-ridden vision of the world from which the author-narrators of *Trommerne* and *Angst* suffered so acutely. Indeed, as Jörn Vosmar has indicated, it is the lack of anxiety in *Bjergene* which, more than anything else, serves to differentiate it from *Trommerne* and *Angst.*[20]

Two years after the publication of *Angst* (1947),[21] Branner announced that he was at work on a cycle of four stories which were to be collectively entitled *Brændte Skibe* and, as Tom Kristensen writes in his review of *Bjergene*:

. . . one was certain that *Angst* would be included in it, that the basic themes of all four of them would rest on the key words in *Angst:* "I don't know if it is my dreams which shape reality of themselves, or whether it is reality which approaches from outside and penetrates my waking sleep," the basic tenet which H. C. Branner has used to raise his art above realism without, however, forsaking those laws he believes himself to have found in the human psyche and dreams.[22]

For three seasons after he had first promised *Brændte Skibe* this title appeared as forthcoming in publishers' lists and catalogues, but it never appeared. In the meantime, Branner published

Söskende and *Rytteren,* and finally, in 1953, *Anst* and *Bjergene* appeared together under the title *Bjergene* with a short preface. In the preface Branner explained that the remaining two stories intended for the promised cycle had, in the course of writing them, been fused together into a unified novel on which he was currently at work. It was only after some reservation that Branner permitted both *Angst* and *Bjergene* to be published together and, when he at last found it defensible to do so, it was because, as he says in the preface: "together they signify the conclusion of a phase in an authorship, an outpost whence no route leads further forward."

The year before *Bjergene* was published Branner had written a pointedly autobiographical short story entitled *Vandring langs Floden,* which was probably composed at the same time as *Söskende*. Like *Bjergene,* it is the story of a successful author and his wife who return to Germany after the war for a holiday. In this story the author continually reflects on the war years, and both he and his wife have a strong feeling of *déjà vu*:

> But when we came into it we again got that peculiar impression of having been there before. We felt it more strongly than any time.[23]

They are trapped by their past and cannot escape, and the author admits that he must write out the past that lives on within him, but he simply cannot work:

> I didn't know either what I would come to write the next time, and I didn't like to think about it. Something had to be broken down before I could begin to work again. That became clearer and clearer to me, but each time I attempted to think about it, I got the feeling in my body that I should die. Just as if it were necessary to die, so that something could live on—something, I didn't know what.[24]

Tarjei Vesaas, Branner's friend and colleague, once stated that Branner often suffered long periods of writer's paralysis, periods in which he saw his typewriter as a many-toothed monster staring up at him.[25] During these periods he worked extremely slowly and had to force himself to compose anything at all. *Angst* and *Bjergene* are probably products of such periods, and *Vandring langs Floden* may disclose the impulses which were to drive him

The End of a Phase and Ingen kender Natten

finally to complete the final two stories for *Brændte Skibe*, the last phase of a stage in his career. As this story is autobiographical in content, it also contains evidence to support the view that the crises in both *Angst* and *Bjergene* were the author's own. Incidentally, it is important to note here that these stories, together with *Trommerne*, probably represent crises of "influence." All three attest to a great deal of influence from Franz Kafka, and, as we have noted, Branner was in the process of translating Kafka's *The Trial* and *The Castle* at relatively the same time as he may have been at work on these stories. Note, too, that Branner himself has freely confessed that Kafka had a very deep influence on his style.[26]

Brændte Skibe is certainly a fitting title for the work which concludes a phase in a Scandinavian author's career, for, as Emil Frederiksen has pointed out,[27] this is also the title of a well-known poem by Ibsen wherein he indicates that he will return to Scandinavia and thus conclude a stage in his career. In this poem Ibsen tells how his thoughts constantly turn from the sunny lands of the Mediterranean to the cold north from which he had come:

> Toward the snowland's cabins
> From the sun strand's thicket
> Rides a rider
> Every single night.[28]

This poem also expresses how, as Branner writes in *Vandring langs Floden*, his thoughts kept returning to the war years, no matter how much he tried to concentrate his thoughts on other things. The author in this story constantly feels that he must say something about personal suffering and moral anxiety against the backdrop of the German occupation. Branner finally did so in *Ingen kender Natten* (1955), which probably represents a fusion of the two final stories originally intended for *Brændte Skibe*. The title, *Ingen kender Natten*, was first used in 1952, when Branner had a fragment of the forthcoming novel published in *Ord och bild*.[29] This fragment is from the section of the novel in which fourteen-year-old Lydia directs thirteen-year-old Simon in his first sexual experience. As Branner rarely read criticism, it is extremely unlikely that he wanted a critical appraisal of this fragment to thereby gauge how the completed novel would be accepted. It seems more reasonable to assume that he published it in order to reassure both himself and his public that he was, in fact, following through with what was to become the major work of his career.

In order to give a clearer picture of the impulses which led to the composition of *Ingen kender Natten,* it seems advisable to outline those works in chronological order which touch upon the war years and the crises of conscience Branner may have undergone as a result of his experiences during those years:

1942 *Trommerne*
1944 *Angst* (First published in the illegal anthology, *Der brænder en Ild.* Legal edition 1945. Has only the title in common with the later work.)
(circa) *Sidst i August*
1945 *Digteren og Pigen* (Though not connected with the war, it reflects some of the difficulties an author has in maintaining a dichotomy between his private life and his work.)
Translated Kafka's *The Trial*
1946 *Die Krise des Humanismus* (The lecture which Branner gave while on tour in Germany.)
At work on *Bjergene*
Jeg ved en Fuglerede in *Ekstrabladets kronik* (October 1, 1946) and republished in *Dansk Udsyn* (1954) and *Vandring langs Floden* (1956). (Tells of his difficulties in working and of reading Sartre's *Huis Clos.*)
1947 *Angst*
Döden varer saa længe. Published in *Vandring langs Floden* (1956). (Tells of Branner's lecture tour in Germany and relates many of the same experiences which the Claus of 1946 had in *Bjergene.*)
1949 Translated Kafka's *The Castle*
1951 *Söskende.* Premiere at Kungliga dramatiska teatern, Stockholm, December 13. (Tells of the war's effect on Michael.)
At work on *Bjergene*
1952 Fragment of *Ingen kender Natten* published in *Ord och Bild.*
1953 *Bjergene*
1955 *Ingen kender Natten.* First appears in the shops on December 5, 1955.

The End of a Phase and Ingen kender Natten

Ingen kender Natten is indisputably Branner's masterpiece and the crowning achievement of his technical and stylistic skills. Its background and logical frame of reference are the last year of the German occupation, but the occupation provides nothing more than a background, for the novel's themes are timeless. In this novel we again meet such typically Branneresque devices as inner monologues, flashbacks, and parallel scenes. Technique is, however, only the procedural aspect of Branner's art, and the importance of *Ingen kender Natten* is its message: the necessity of accepting an other-directed communal responsibility as a sort of ethical imperative. Acceptance of this imperative may, to be sure, mean the loss of one's life, but, so the novel leads us to believe, the loss of one's life in accepting this imperative is but to gain it. To isolate this imperative as the life-giving force, all else must be negated, annihilated, or relegated to the realm of worthless values. All else must, as Tomas says, become empty thoughts and words.

We can best describe the pattern of *Ingen kender Natten* by drawing an analogy with chess. The novel falls into two parts: 1) Simon's flight from the Gestapo and Tomas's conversations inside Gabriel's villa and 2) the story of Simon and Tomas and their joint activity in the warehouse. In both sections the pattern is stitched together by two essential narrative threads which are almost inextricably intermingled and woven together. The threads are carried by members of two teams, one of which is led by Simon and the other by Tomas. The two move closer and closer together until they clash, and the piece from one side is captured by the piece from the other. The Simon narrative is the narrative of the black team, for it is Simon who wanders about alone in the dark night outside the luminous headquarters of the white team, Tomas's team. These two narratives are so skillfully spliced together that, as in *Bjergene*, the end of a speech by a member of one team may be continued without interruption by a member of the other team. The most meaningful example of this technique occurs at the end of the first section. Simon, chased by the Gestapo, finally arrives outside the villa, and, in his mental and physical exhaustion, he says: "Get up," and the next section begins with Tomas's repetition of this phrase. In this way Simon's physical immobility is related to Tomas's paralysis of will. However, after they have met, Simon confers his will to act upon Tomas, so that Tomas and Simon actually exchange places and Tomas becomes a primary mover in the underground. The pattern of the novel forms an hourglass. Simon is distracted from his task by his inability to move toward his goal, and he ends by suffering from the paralysis of will with which Tomas began. The novel's rhythm is thus formed of pulsating, interconnected narratives which give the illusion of simultaneity to the separate actions of Simon and Tomas.

Many of the themes present in Branner's other works crop up once again in *Ingen kender Natten,* but here they reappear in a much more concentrated form. In fact, one can almost read the novel as a summation of the various themes and concepts which together compose his artistic world. The novel's title is an oblique reference to Ingemann's poem, *Ingen kender Dagen,* often used at children's funerals.[30] Simplistically, one can infer that the title signifies that no man knows the night, knows what dark mysteries life holds until dawn breaks, when he may finally see a vision of hope and understanding:

> But the innermost meaning must be the mystery of life, the secretive living dark where life and death are woven together, where life is continually renewed in eternity, the hidden and unconscious bond between people.[31]

At the conclusion of the novel Tomas sees a vision of light and hope as he hears the tones of Grundtvig's hymn, *Den signede Dag,* from Frelserkirken.[32] This is a morning song about an eternal light, a light which continues in spite of the dark, signifying that life continues in spite of death. It is this contrast between light and dark which continually interests Branner, not only in *Ingen kender Natten,* but throughout his career.[33] Light is constantly played off against dark so that nothing is apprehended in a fixed way, but is constantly shifted between these two extremes and is never absolute.

At the very outset of the novel we meet the Communist resistance leader, Simon (presumably named after Simon the Zealot, the Hebrew patriot), who is in flight from the Gestapo. Since puberty he has been obsessed with the thin, red-haired Lydia, who seduced him when he was thirteen.[34] As a child, like so many of Branner's girl figures, she represented the Queen of Evil to him

The End of a Phase and Ingen kender Natten

and terrorized him.[35] After having seduced him, she was taken away by the authorities and he was punished by his strict and severely religious father who placed him in a dark coal cellar.[36] Just three days before the novel opens, Simon had met her near Langebro after they had been separated for some months. She is a German camp follower, and as a member of the resistance his relationship with her is mortally dangerous for him. He is now in flight from her apartment, for he fears that she has sent the Gestapo for him. Their affair has been a love-hate relationship. Her mother had been the district whore, and she is filled with a masochistic sense of self-contempt and deprecation. She is totally incapable of pulling herself out of her social rut.[37] Simon is tired of being an instrument to abet her masochism, and she mocks his protests by calling him "priest" and "missionary." When he accuses her of dancing with the Germans, she does a little German boot dance before him. Branner again turns to the image of the dancing, mocking girl when Sonja and Daphne are forced to dance around Felix in order to stimulate him sexually.[38] At a first reading this near repetition of scene may incite no more than a dim echo in the reader's mind. Nevertheless, Simon is well aware of the similarities, and this is what strikes him when he first glimpses Daphne through the window of Gabriel's villa:

> An insect, he thought, and followed her light rhythmic dance down the steps side by side with the short grotesque cavalier, a shiny silver-gray moth to be squeezed to death between two fingers and blown away like dust, like nothing, a glimmer of nothing and just the same—just the same. Like Lydia, he thought amazed, do I want her just the same as I want Lydia? And via a sudden, unreasonable connection of thoughts he saw Lydia slowly sink forward with a little circular hole in the small cleft in the nape of her neck.[39]

In an instant of fitful passion, Simon makes love to Lydia in her apartment; a fleeting moment of love and hate, after which he feels only emptiness. Then, in the terror of his flight, he imagines that she is not guilty for having caused him to flee, but that he alone is to blame.[40] Tomas, whom Simon sees inside Gabriel's villa, is pondering the same problem; the problem of personal responsibility for guilt. In this way the two are mentally related. Both are related physically as well. Simon is completely exhausted after his flight, and he feels that he cannot get up and continue his flight.

Inside the villa Tomas has drunk himself into a stupor, and he feels that he cannot get up. At the end of Chapter One, Simon says:

"Onward," he said and remained sitting. "Get up," he said and remained sitting.—[41]

and at the beginning of the next chapter, Tomas says:

"Get up," Tomas said to himself and remained sitting.[42]

Just as Simon's thoughts have dissolved into a disjunctive jumble in which past and present are inextricably mingled, so Tomas's thoughts have also become disoriented, and everything has become a meaningless jumble of words:

"Oh, holy hocus-pocus of words," said Tomas, "stay out of my life with your idiotic cabal of sexual symbols. I am not playing along any more." [43]

Tomas's mind is split into disparate entities, as is symbolized by his name, which means "twins." His name is also divisible into *Tom* and *Mads*. Gabriel calls him Tom, while Daphne calls him Mads, suggesting the role of a clown.[44] Essentially, though, he is the doubting Thomas, the pondering prober of the mind. He is a disbelieving skeptic vis-à-vis illusions, and this is shown at the very outset when he reflects on a childhood experience.[45] Once when he had attended a performance, a hypnotist had made an entire room of adults believe that the room was filled with a swarm of bees. Only he, a child, was not duped; but at the very thought of the experience, he now lifts his hands to ward off the bees. The process of mental dissolution has advanced so far that even his rational skepticism has been broken down.

Tomas holds himself responsible for his mother's death, and, although she actually committed suicide, he has an abiding sense of guilt.[46] He believes that he could have called for a doctor or could have saved her in some way, and he reproaches himself for merely having stood by while she died. His mother had tried everything possible to bind her son to her. She refused to permit

The End of a Phase and Ingen kender Natten

him to play with other children. She tried to buy his affection by giving him gifts of animals, but he always let them die.[47] She got him drunk when he was fourteen and then told him that: "she believed that sexual union was the meaning and goal of everything."[48] Finally, when she died, he discovered that the creature who had terrorized him and dominated him was nothing more than a painted-up child.[49] Tomas totally rejected and hated his mother, and a Freudian interpretation would undoubtedly suggest that his rejection was the result of an inverted Oedipus complex, though Tomas himself denies this.[50] His sense of guilt is the essential condition for all of his emotional responses.[51] The inner monologue in which he discusses these matters is couched in the language of the confessional. At one point he even looks under the table to see if a priest is present, and in his mind the image of a priest is associated with that of a clown.[52] His sense of guilt is so intense that the prospect of forgiveness held out by organized religion is reduced to a comedy of manners. Despite reflection and rationalization, he simply cannot absolve himself of the vision of his dead mother; he cannot divest himself of guilt and anxiety. Tomas's inner monologue is then interrupted by Simon's, and his thoughts are also preoccupied with religion:

> I am a bad boy and Jesus is mad at me. I am a bad boy and Jesus is mad at me. I am a bad boy and Jesus is mad at me. I am a, no Jesus is a bad . . . no, it wasn't defiance, but he had already said it many hundreds of times and couldn't help it if he got confused at the last. Oh, Jesus, help!"[53]

Simon, like Börge in *Historien om Börge,* has projected the father upon the world and arrived at the idea of God, for he, too, has replaced the image of God with the image of his father. As his father frustrated his wishes and punished him, his negative conception of his father is reflected in his attitude toward God, for he sees him solely as the author of prohibitive commands.

In their reflective consciousnesses both Simon and Tomas repeatedly try to gain a vision of the truth and a clearer realization of themselves. In this they are unique, for none of the other characters in the novel are committed to such a process, and their commitment further unites them as "soul mates." Nevertheless, both are doomed to failure in their attempts, just as Claus in *Bjergene* and the author-narrators of *Trommerne* and *Angst* are doomed to failure. As Jörn Vosmar states:

> Any search for truth is doomed to become a meaningless play upon words. If one cultivates that game, he soon finds himself on the bounds of reason. And Branner cultivates it in his books, *must* cultivate it. Therefore, the course of development runs from the first novels' "normal" people to Claus in *Bjergene* and Tomas in *Ingen kender Natten*, where both have passed the bounds. It is mad, drunk and dead tired people who speak in Branner's later books. Therefore, the old-fashioned narrative point of view in *Legetöj* is replaced by an endless stream of consciousness and colossal monologues. Form and content have disintegrated.[54]

There are further indications that Claus in *Bjergene* and Tomas are related. Tomas, like Claus, is an author who plays with words, and he describes himself as a poet of advertising.[55]

Both Claus and Tomas describe themselves as fearless, and both refer to the fairy tale about the man who set out to know fear and discovered its meaning only after his wife had poured a bucket of sticklebacks over him.[56]

Simon's observations of the actions inside the villa are interrupted by Tomas's inner observations, his stream of consciousness.[57] In these passages Tomas, too, is revealed as a silent observer who watches Daphne and her father as they play together like children:

> They constantly play the same game as when she was a little girl: he is the teddy bear who crawls on all fours before her on the carpet. She twitches his ears and tugs his hair and beard. They bump into each other's foreheads and call each other meaningless names.[58]

Gabriel has preserved Daphne as a child and has kept her locked within herself. She, like Lord Monchesy's son Harry in T. S. Eliot's *The Family Reunion,* is the product of her father's failure to face his own passions. Just as Gabriel has refused to live and develop fully and has locked himself within his own system of ideas, so he wants to prevent his daughter from developing fully. Daphne actually hates her father for his repressions and for his treatment of her mother, and Gabriel is well aware of her hate.[59]

The End of a Phase and Ingen kender Natten

Daphne's counterpart is Sonja. In the following chapter,[60] Tomas converses with her and her impotent and perverse lover, Dr. Felix.

Dr. Felix begins his conversation with Tomas with a flow of psychoanalytical terms, and Tomas calls him his brother.[61] In at least one sense, Felix is Tomas's brother, for Tomas has been under psychiatric care and understands the implications of the terms which both he and Felix use; there is merely a verbal bond of fraternity between them. Tomas realizes that the terms themselves are meaningless jargon used for a sort of ritual which is to ease the pain of the mind's larger concerns:

Paranoid, schizoid, ixoid, delusions. There is something deeply reassuring about these foreign psychiatric words; that is if one doesn't think too much about their content—yes, it's actually best if one doesn't think at all and doesn't understand the words but merely lets their magic affect one.[62]

Felix, the well manicured, suave, athletic lover, regards love as a ritual act, as something which, at length, loses its meaning. Having heard Felix's *ars amatoria*, Tomas conjures forth an image of the great lover's home, his temple of love.[63] He imagines it as a luxuriously appointed apartment with a mirror in which Felix and his lovers are reflected and fitted with:

. . . an automatic record player, and while the banal melody with its eternally same motif toiled round and round at a snail's pace. . . .[64]

Felix finally admits that he is attracted to the frigid virginal, inexperienced woman, and the first indication of his impotency is thereby exposed.[65] Felix is really like a young boy who compulsively describes imagined sexual conquests to reassure his more experienced comrades that he is actually part of the group. Tomas finally hears the truth about Felix when he talks to Sonja who tells him about Felix's impotence and perversion.[66] She also confirms Tomas's imagined version of Felix's temple of love as a piece of reality, even in the detail of the mirror.

Having concluded his conversations with Felix and Sonja, Tomas then talks to his father-in-law, and their conversation is constantly interrupted by flashbacks to Simon, who is still waiting outside the villa. Simon finally enters as Tomas's conversation with Gabriel ends with Gabriel's death.[67] Gabriel is a greatly expanded version of the Copenhagen financier whom we met in *Sidste Skib*,[68] and he also has certain affinities with Feddersen in *Legetöj*, Herman in *Rytteren*, Carl Björndal in *Drömmen om en Kvinde*, Irene's husband in *Söskende*, and Henry, whom we are to meet later in *Thermopylæ*. All are exponents of the Nazi spirit, but Gabriel is distinguished by the fact that he represents a threat to democracy from within. He is for disenfranchisement of the individual, for he wishes to control the individual by the medium of advertising.[69] He wants to conduct opinion research and construct a super propaganda machine of advertising that will convince the individual that what Gabriel wants is what he wants. Gabriel describes himself as a faithless, sick old man who all his life has sought to accumulate money and things and he admits that he has suffered acutely from this curse.[70] It is, in fact, things "which have estranged me from people; people have, as it were, become things." Gabriel has become a victim of the materialistic hell he wishes to impose upon others. For him, everything is an object which can be bought and sold, and it is only logical that people also become marketable objects. He has tried to satisfy his wife by providing her with things; but she has, he suggests, found revenge for his solely material response by drowning herself.[71] Trapped in a hell of his own making, he sees Tomas as his only means of escape.[72] In this he reminds us of Susanne in *Rytteren* who was begged for support from Herman and Michala. However, Tomas, like Susanne, is in no condition to help anyone; at least, not until he can be radically transformed into something else.

Outside the villa Simon has sent out a cry into the night:

Someone must help me now there must be a person somewhere something must happen now—now—.[73]

Finally, something does happen inside the villa. Gabriel's lengthy monologue is suddenly broken off when he falls to the floor. He has had the heart attack he has feared for so long. Tomas gets up and bends over Gabriel on the floor. He then discovers that everything about Gabriel is false: he has dyed his hair, his teeth are false.[74] Tomas smiles at the sight, since this is precisely the same discovery he made after his mother died. He bends over

The End of a Phase and Ingen kender Natten

and kisses Gabriel on the forehead and senses a deep tenderness.[75] Tomas has begun to feel, and he notes that the kiss seems to have awakened the dying face to a new life:

> But it didn't become a smile. The face became dark and drew itself into knots. There came a weak, whimpering sound. Then crying followed, an almost inaudible cry, like that of a child who has cried and cried until it no longer has the voice left to cry. Tomas had to smile, since he had listened to that tiny despairing cry the whole time. At that moment it rose from the deep like the sound in a dying person's mouth, a spasm in a dying face, but it had been there the whole time. He had heard it behind all of Gabriel's capers, behind Daphne's silver bell voice with its small empty words, behind Felix, the lover's fraudulent gestures, behind the girlish Sonja's hastily dancing stream of talk. All night long he had sat and listened to it; in fact not just that night, but many nights, all the nights back to his childhood.[76]

Tomas has been listening to the cries of petulant children; all those inside the villa represent childish regressions. It is the cry of a child which also cries out within him. Previously, we have noted that, when one of Branner's characters recognizes the cry of a child within himself, then he is soon to undergo a spiritual transformation.[77] It is not only the imagined cry of a child which Tomas hears, but also the cry of Daphne as she sees her father dead on the floor.

Just as Gabriel has fallen to the floor, the servant Marie has dropped a dish and cries out at the sight of Simon, who has finally entered the villa. Tomas goes out to see what has caused the disturbance and meets Simon and hails him as his brother. His greeting marks the conclusion of the first part of *Ingen kender Natten* and of his passivity. Tomas has risen to act and has been transformed into a participant in the lives of others. Nevertheless, he is still obsessed with the same sense of guilt as previously, and it is only in the final section of the novel that he absolves himself of that guilt.

Having recognized each other as brothers, Simon and Tomas talk together while Tomas cares for Simon's wounds.[78] Simon then takes Tomas into his confidence and asks for his help. He tells him of his activities in the underground and that he is on the way to a group of fugitives who have sought refuge in a warehouse. Finally, Tomas agrees to drive him to the warehouse, and he gets

Simon into a car and sets out for the warehouse. On the way they are stopped at a German check point, and Tomas uses his linguistic and acting ability to get through, so that they arrive safely at their destination. This section of the novel is related in conventional narrative form; the use of stream of consciousness is suppressed. It is only at the conclusion of this section that a return to this technique occurs. When Tomas enters the warehouse he again hears a child's cry, but this time it is not an illusion. It is the baby of one of the fugitives. Realism has begun to supplant illusion, but just at the moment it begins to do so, Tomas is hit over the head and falls to the floor of the warehouse.

Tomas's passivity has now been transformed into an active unending search, a search to explain himself to himself, to account for his actions. Symbolically enough, just as Tomas sets out in the car with Simon, he utters a statement in direct contradiction to Christ's words in the Sermon on the Mount:

"He who seeks shall not find. He who asks for meaning has already uttered a meaningless question. We should be glad about that, for it's a great solace." [79]

This statement may be interpreted to signify that Tomas has divorced his quest from any implications of Christian charity and that he demands no larger meaning be attached to his quest. It is the spontaneity of his actions which are significant, not their causal relation to some meaningful goal; and this is a conceptualized expression of his almost existential freedom to act.

Previously, Tomas had concerned himself with the apparent meaninglessness of words, just as the author-narrators in *Trommerne* and *Angst* and Claus in *Bjergene* had concerned themselves with the same problem, a problem which is essential for them to resolve. While in the car, Tomas suddenly turns to Simon and says:

No, don't ask about anything. We will not touch sacrosanct things. We will not flee from them by demanding a meaning from them. Let nice meaningless words be what they are. Let us believe they mean the same; life and death one and the same.[80]

From these statements we conclude that nothing but the search for some view of the truth and meaning about himself now mat-

The End of a Phase and Ingen kender Natten

ters to Tomas. He has taken on an abstract, almost mystical approach to life, an approach which makes it unnecessary that the expressive units of reality, words, have meaning. Previously, he has looked for some sign, some word that would put an end to his world of illusions and give him a clear definition of his life. Like Claus Böje in *Barnet leger ved Stranden* he has sought an absolute definition of truth and reality, but also like Claus, he realizes that such a definition is impossible. There is, however, one important difference between Claus Böje and Tomas. Tomas has come to realize that a search for absolutes is not only impossible, but, more important to his mystical approach to life, it is not even necessary.

While Tomas lies unconscious in the warehouse, the fugitives begin to argue among themselves and all their petty differences come creeping out. Finally, a priest—almost a reincarnation of the priest Tomas had imagined earlier—stands up and addresses his fellows on the concepts of guilt and responsibility:

. . . "it's correct for us to keep the spirit of humanism alive. It's right that one should fight for his fatherland, and it's right that the fight today is the only necessity—all of that's correct. But we're forgetting the most important thing: responsibility, the individual's responsibility for the common cause." [81]

However, the searching, doubting Tomas is still obsessed with a sense of guilt, and he cannot finally accept the other-directed communal responsibility the priest mentions until he meets Lene.

Lene, who is helping the fugitives, is a stepchild. As a child she had been forced into prostitution by her stepfather. Now that he is old and helpless, she cares for him and feels driven to the task by her own sense of guilt.[82] As opposed to Lydia, Sonja, and Daphne, she is the only positive female figure in the novel. Her full name, Martha Maria Magdalene, signifies that she is a female archetype of almost mythical proportions, at once mother, sister, wife, and whore.[83] Her instinct tells her that she must help Tomas, and she does so by making love to him, reincarnating him into a new life:

She laughed and cried with joy. Warm rain fell on his face. "Now I'm your mother," she whispered, "now I love you, now I take you. I take you back again. Can you feel it, completely inside me? Now you don't exist; you're inside me. And now—now I give birth to you. . . ."[84]

Lene's reincarnation and regeneration of Tomas effect the final stage of his transformation from an ineffectual, passive observer to an active person who accepts an other-directed communal responsibility. The change is slightly fantastic, given the facts that Tomas has been drinking all night, is under tremendous physical and psychological pressure, and is close to the brink of exhaustion. Surely this rebirth must be seen as largely symbolic. The theme of psychological rebirth, transformation, and regeneration by intercourse is in keeping with the ideas of other contemporary Scandinavian authors, such as Johan Borgen and Sigurd Hoel.[85] Nevertheless, Tomas's final transformation permits him to take part in an activity which is larger than life and death. As he falls in a hail of German bullets while covering the fugitives' retreat, Tomas evokes an essential tenet of Branner's *Weltanschauung:* to lose one's life is but to gain it. It is the same lesson which the dying Mortimer learned in *Drömmen om en Kvinde* while alone in his hotel room.

Ingen kender Natten stands as a summation of the themes, images, and symbols recurrent in Branner's other works, but it is unique in its striking note of prophetic moral judgment: one must confront reality, adapt oneself to it in accepting it, and, should the ethical exigencies of reality and moral choice so demand it, one must lose oneself in order to gain oneself. The novel places the eternal clash between private and social values into an ethical perspective. Tomas's claustration of the soul, his denial of communal responsibility, is broken when he accepts Simon's telepathically communicated plea for help. The telepathic communication of such a message is also a basic theme in Kjeld Abell's *De blaa Pekingeser,* and it is interesting to note that Branner felt more personally involved in this play than any other of Abell's works. Branner even prepared a radio version of this play. Thus, in Branner's last novel the humanistic imperative of accepting communal responsibility is prophetically advanced in answer to the dilemma posed by an insistence on absolute personal freedom within the context of social demands.

CHAPTER 6

Drama and Short Story once more

ONE year after the publication of *Ingen kender Natten*, Branner published the autobiographical collection of essays entitled *Vandring langs Floden*.[1] These essays provide glimpses into the events, ideas, and crises that had shaped his career from circa 1939 through 1956. As we have mentioned these essays from time to time in the course of our review of his other works, it is not necessary to do so once more, but we should make some general statement about the collection as a whole. Most of the essays are told in the first person, but it is not H. C. Branner's "I" alone that is speaking, rather it is the "I" of an artist who reflects the difficult and tumultuous period in which he was writing. Taken together, these essays evoke a tragicomic note of an author concerned with his supersensitivity, his insights, and his successes or failures as a positive interpreter of his *Zeitgeist*. Most of the essays, as we have seen, have rather specific connections with his individual works. For example, as Emil Frederiksen suggests,[2] *Et grædende Barn* apparently contains a sketch of Tomas in the first part of *Ingen kender Natten*. Be that as it may, at least one sentence in this piece seems to summarize Tomas's attitude before he meets Simon:

> I am a person adrift, torn loose from past and future; I exist only in the instant which surges up straight from the deep like a mad sea, created by God knows what contradictions.[3]

and another summarizes the effect Lene has on Tomas:

> . . . but my mind no longer has the rich formlessness of the clouds. It has begun to stiffen into definite figures like ice flowers on a window pane.[4]

143

In his review of *Vandring langs Floden*, Tom Kristensen notes that Branner had revealed himself to be much more than the humanist he had so often been labeled:

> With such engaging prose H. C. Branner reveals one of his secrets. It is not enough to simplify a great artist by placing the label "humanist" on him. He is more; he is much more. He is a whirlpool who casts out portrayals of human beings.[5]

Though the essays in *Vandring langs Floden* reflect Branner's attitude toward his work and himself through 1956, it was the political events of that year which were to prompt him to make a statement on the position of art and the artist in the postwar world. On October 21–23 demonstrations occurred in Hungary, and the crowds were fired upon. Six days later it was announced that Soviet troops would leave Hungary and appeals were made to the rebels to cease fire, because they had won. But the revolution continued, until early on the morning of November 4 Russian artillery opened fire on Budapest and Soviet tanks entered the city. When order was finally restored, 7,000 Russian troops and 30,000 Hungarian citizens were dead. Hungary was an occupied country, and a puppet régime had been set up under János Kádár. As a result of these events European intellectuals and Communist sympathizers underwent a crisis of conscience. Many were deeply disaffected by the brutality of the Russian suppression of the Hungarians. Not untypically, the Icelandic Nobel laureate Halldór Laxness went so far as to write a letter of protest to Khrushchev. These were the events which prompted Branner to deliver a speech on the position of art and the artist in times of political turmoil at the Danish Student Union in Copenhagen on November 24, 1956.

Branner's lecture, *Kunstens Uafhængighed* (*The Independence of Art*),[6] not only offers important suggestions as to the place of art and the artist in society, but it also contains statements relevant to a better understanding of many of the ideas in Branner's works. At the outset he defines his attitude toward an absolutist interpretation of truth, freedom and justice:

> The great ideal concepts—words like truth, freedom, and justice—are aspects of the ideas of mankind, and they only have significance

within this context. The truth only permits itself to be defined as the greatest possible agreement between the greatest possible number of factors—absolute truth does not exist, unless one is induced to a religious train of thoughts. Absolute freedom is the same as absolute meaninglessness, for human beings are only human beings by force of numberless states of dependence, and justice carried out as an absolute principle would very quickly lead to inhumanity.[7]

Throughout his authorship Branner continually denies the validity of the absolutist view. Claus Böje in *Barnet leger ved Stranden* finally realizes that, within the shifting, ever mutable context of reality, absolute truths are inconceivable. This is the same conclusion reached by the author narrators in *Trommerne* and *Angst*, as well as by Claus in *Bjergene*. An author must continually search to redefine reality,[8] and he cannot, therefore, confine himself to any one faith or set of principles:

It occurs to me that development has shown that, just as it has shown that artistic freedom is a necessary condition for interaction between the individual and society. Therefore, as an artist, I cannot permit myself to be bound by any one belief or doctrine. I cannot bring people the truth, because the truth is not something fixed, but something which must continually be sought anew.[9]

In passing Branner states that he is primarily concerned with the psychology of the individual.[10] However, the fundamental article of faith enunciated in this essay is the necessity for a persistent iterative commitment to a redefinition of the major concepts of reality: truth, freedom and justice, as well as his emphasis on the value of the individual as opposed to the mass. The categorical necessity for a continual search to redefine these values makes it imperative for Branner to preserve an artistic independence if he is to be an independent interpreter of the spirit of his times—a demand which was also made by the author-narrators of *Trommerne* and *Angst*. That is, if he is to succeed as an impartial observer, then he must remain independent and aloof. Art and politics have nothing to do with each other.[11] The task of the artist is to stand as an expression of the conscience of the era in which he works; this is his sole responsibility. In accepting it, he must keep himself open to different opinions about empirical facts; and this is a concern which lies at the very heart of the ideas Branner presents in *Kunstens Uafhængighed*. The artistic realization of this concern is a collage of attitudes, rather than a fixed set of beliefs. This essay is, then, a policy statement of the conceptual and formal requisites Branner has set on his art: it should take the form of an incessant search for renewal, a search to continually rechart an imaginative vision of perception. Branner's philosophical position is agnostic and existential, and it is therefore only natural that the quest motif occupies a central position in his art. The context of that quest is continually shifting, but the objective is always the same: truth. Just as the quest is an essential element of myth, so many of Branner's works take on mythical proportions and take place in a world above or prior to ordinary time, a world where the distinctions between past, present and future are sporadically lost. They are, in Northrop Frye's terminology, fables of identity.

A negative stand can be taken to Branner's view of artistic independence. It can be asserted that absolute independence is just as self-destructive and unobtainable as absolute truth, freedom, or justice. If the artist does not take a definite stand on some issue, then he runs the risk of committing the crime of silence. However, what Branner is essentially arguing against in his essay is something which ethical philosophers call the "naturalistic fallacy." This consists in identifying ethical concepts, such as justice and freedom, with certain natural properties, such as "more evolved," or "according to the Western view of life." In order to avoid this fallacy the artist must hold himself independent of making such definitions and seek out the meaning of freedom and justice within the context of life. In short, Branner is saying that the artist must remain above the immediacy and contemporaneity which often effect naturalistic definitions of ethical properties. He must remain objective and not associate subjective, naturalistic values with ethical properties.

Some two weeks before Branner delivered his lecture, Danish radio audiences had heard his sixth radio play, *Jeg elsker dig*.[12] This play relates the consequences of a chance meeting of three couples. August Bloch, a middle-aged lawyer, and his wife, Leonora, have led a stiflingly bourgeois existence. Their home is crowded with heavy mahogany furniture and Copenhagen porcelain. David, a twenty-two-year-old law student, is in love with Clara, another Klara Kvistgaard. André is a con man and charmer of professional proportions, and he is married to Vivian, a second-rate actress. All six meet by chance at a restaurant after they have seen the same film. Their only connection with one another is that Clara works for August Bloch, and August knows André by reputation only. Under the influence of a few drinks and the intoxicating atmosphere of the restaurant, they soon find themselves playing musical chairs. Motherly Leonora becomes infatuated with David's youthful innocence. André attempts to charm Clara and is attracted by her virginity. Fatherly August falls victim to Vivian's charms. Their conversations are blended and spliced together into a harmonic pattern until the restaurant closes and they must return home. They return home paired off as they came and, once they arrive back at their respective homes, they each find that the evening's emotionally charged experiences nearly cause them to break up with each other. Finally, however, they come to terms with each other. Leonora discovers that she cannot live without her fatherly August, and he confesses that he loves his motherly Leonora. Vivian discovers that she enjoys André's brutality and slick charm. Clara takes the initiative and leads David off to bed.

This play is little more than an interesting example of tightly knit composition and a study in contrast. It contains nothing of the penetrating character analysis in Branner's more serious works, nor is it concerned with the problems of defining truth and reality as do Branner's major works from the late forties and early fifties. It stands alone as one of the least successful dramatic works of his artistic maturity.

Branner's last stage play, *Thermopylæ*,[13] was produced at Copenhagen's Royal Theater in 1958 and was unfavorably reviewed by the critics; this initial reaction has not been altered by subsequent revivals. *Thermopylæ* is a supernaturalistic chamber play in four acts. Act I takes place on September 30, 1938, the day of the Munich Pact. Act II is set in October, 1939, after the outbreak of the war, and the two final acts take place on a winter day toward the end of the war. The drama is centered around Stefan Fischer, a highly cultivated humanist and professor of classical history who in Act II has just published a book entitled *Thermopylæ* and his family. In its exposure of the political and ideological tensions of the outside world by reference to the microcosm of the family as a mirror of those tensions the play is strongly reminiscent of Eugene O'Neill. This identification is even more suitable when one notes that both authors used reiterative phrases as verbal symbols to suggest inevitability and fate. "Reality, the real life" are the reiterative verbal keys of *Thermopylæ,* and characterization is conducted by contrasting the varied and varying reactions to and interpretations of this concept.[14] Stefan's ideal of reality is humanism defined as antiauthoritarianism, i.e. freedom; but he is not ideally free, for he is insistent on remaining true to his ideals. In the face of Nazi oppression Stefan remains true to his humanistically defined conception of the real life and in the process he destroys the lives of those about him. As the play's dominant figure Stefan reveals a heroic, superhuman steadfastness to his ideals which ultimately leads to martyrdom. Stefan has dominated the lives of his two sons, Axel, who becomes a Nazi, and Kai, who becomes a Communist. Both have embraced absolutist views of the real life which represent controverted interpretations of Stefan's humanism. Kai, whose name refers to Cain, finally kills Axel, whose name refers to Abel. In terms of nominal morphology and symbolism they are either tragically incomplete or garbled reflections of the ideals Stefan professes. The biblical symbolism is complete when we note that Stefan refers to the first Christian martyr. Stefan has also attempted to control the lives of his wife, Anna, and his daughter, Helene. He has desperately wanted Helene to employ her eroticism in effecting a psychic cure for Kristoffer, the artist who lives with Stefan and whom he regards as a visionary savior. Kristoffer is another Michael, and Helene ultimately rejects him for Henry, who is another Gabriel. Anna and Helene subsequently leave Stefan, as does his secretary, Barbara, a sort of Berta figure. On her way out Barbara tells Stefan the real effect his preaching and ideals have had on the lives nearest him:

BARBARA: Kai was right. You are a self-deceiver. Now I can see it. You talk about reality—but you have no idea what real life is all about. You believe in human charity and love—but your love has killed the people around you.[15]

Thus, in *Thermopylæ,* as in *Söskende,* we learn that absolute justice leads to absolute injustice, because it is inhuman; and in *Thermopylæ,* too, we have a condemnation of the idealist as a dialectician solely interested in the absolute view of reality, a view totally lacking in human values. Stefan is an expression of the danger of humanism, for he is a humanist unaware of humanity.

Thermopylæ suffers from overwriting and undercharacterization. It is all too obviously written to have an esthetic existence, but its chief fault is overdependency on Stefan as a vector of intellectual abstractions alone. There is no dramatic foundation to direct our sympathies toward him, and the play thereby disintegrates into tragi-comedy. Stefan is Molière's Alceste or Ibsen's Gregers Werle and Rosmer combined. The positively "good" man is an other-worldly, unreal abstraction which becomes comic when placed in the real world. That is the clownish aspect of Clemens as a doer of good deeds. By placing Stefan in a world bounded by the terror and oppression of Nazism, Branner had attempted the superhuman task of making Stefan "real." He failed for the same reasons Dostoevski failed to make Prince Myshkin real in *The Idiot*: he insisted on remaining a realist throughout a supernaturalistic play, and *Thermopylæ* stands as Branner's least successful theatrical effort.

On New Year's Day 1959 Branner held a talk entitled *En Nytårsklokke*,[16] on Danish radio. This talk is a deeply personal reflection on what the advent of the new year meant to Branner. He reflects on the changing seasons as he wanders by the seashore. When he was young, he says, he felt nature immediately and keenly and not, as in later life, as something which could only be internalized via intellectual apprehension. In the winter the child knew that the flowers were beneath the snow and vaguely understood that: "in the mystery of death one found one's mysterium of life." [17] Branner is once again referring to the cycle of nature, the pivot of renewal, most poignantly expressed in *Drömmen om en Kvinde* and *Ingen kender Natten*. In this essay, too, he expands on the meaning of death:

> But he who approaches old age must, in his best moments, nourish the belief that even the decline toward death means growth, a turning back and a beginning.[18]

At the conclusion of the essay he reflects on the chime of church bells he once heard when eleven years old on the day that the First World War began. Those bells rang in war, and war bounded the major phases in his life: the post-, mid- and prewar years. Now, as he recalls the past, he believes that he stands on the threshold of a new beginning:

> Not that one has lost courage. The period of anxiety is over, the flight from reality is no longer possible and doubt has become a meaningless thing. We live in the time of the cold stars, under the law of necessity.[19]

Et Nytårsklokke is related in the delicately lyrical style that was to color much of the production of Branner's remaining six years as an author, and it is clearly noticeable in his next work, *Et Spil om Kærligheden og Döden* (1960).[20]

This radio play is a lyrical tone poem on the themes of love and death. Time is here abstractly conceived, but not separated from the particularity of place and historical change. Voices speak out and blend into the background, and the whole pattern of the drama is infused with a wealth of symbolism. It is an artistic vision of love and death and the sensations of guilt and responsibility, the perpetual conceptual cement of Branner's world. Guilt and responsibility are played off against the demands of love.

In *Et Spil om Kærligheden og Döden* a journalist, who is never named, meets a woman at a banquet held by her husband. Her husband is the typical Branneresque businessman; ruthless, unfeeling, and totally materialistically oriented. He has recently purchased the paper for which the journalist is now to write. The journalist, a resistance fighter, prisoner of war at Sachsenhausen and thereafter a well known reporter from "every sector where freedom was in combat with tyranny," has been purchased outright to ornament the paper with a well-known name. She, the businessman's wife, has been purchased, like Irene in *Söskende*, as an ornament for her husband's desire for power and prestige. She, now thirty-five, has two children: a son, Peter, aged seventeen, and a daughter, aged sixteen, in Switzerland. The journalist's wife is a weak, sensitive woman who has been griefstricken ever since her infant son died. She is consumed by the death wish and wants only to be united with her dead son. The businessman's wife, again like Irene in *Söskende*, is fully aware of the fact that she has been purchased like so much meat, but she wishes only that she can revive her husband from spiritual death. The journalist had

had one driving motive in life: to confront his readers with the truth no one would hear. Thus, both he and she are deeply affected by death in life. His wife is afflicted by the death wish, and her husband is spiritually dead. Having talked together, she decides that she wants to liberate him by giving him the courage to live his own life. Both are on the brink of fleeing from their individual responsibilities into a realm of romantic fantasy. She asks him if he can stop loving his wife, and he replies by defining love as an emotional state in which one shares joys and sorrows, serves one another, and feels secure with one another. Finally, just before they decide to flee together, she recites an ode to the freedom which love offers, a freedom she fervently desires:

I believe nothing. I want nothing. I want only to exist on this earth. To be with the one I love, to love him and know that he loves me. To fall asleep with my arms about him, to awaken to new life together with him, to open my eyes at sunup and see the dew blinking in the grass. To lie under a big tree and listen to it rustling up in the leaves —to exist in that sound, to be like a tree. Like fruit which ripens and falls. Like the birds who fly away with the dark and return with the light. To follow the flight of the clouds, to listen to the wind and the crash of the waves, to close my eyes when I am tired and see the sea before me. To go away and return and feel secure in that. To love life and have enough of it. To believe in life and death because they mean life and death and nothing else.—[21]

The lilting lyrical tone is diffused throughout the remainder of the play and climbs to a peak at the conclusion. It is this lyrical quality which makes the play credible as a tone poem. Under the onslaught of such lyrical passages, the structural framework of the play, its "real" events, slip into the background of the mind, and a symbolic interpretation is imposed. Critically judged, these "real" events disintegrate as credible units. Quite simply, how could two people who have just professed an acute sense of responsibility for those nearest to them suddenly decide to flee after a brief exchange of words were it not for the power of the fantasy of love, the fantasy which is encapsuled in the lyricism of such passages? As in *Trolus and Cressida,* we are confronted with a tone poem of love which is unsatisfactory for the tragedy it attempts because its conclusion is so indefinite. As in Shakespeare's play, there is the same undramatic trailing-off of the sequences of events, the same lack of control over dramatic form. There is an impossible mixture of evil reality—guilt and responsibility lurking in the wings—and lyrical enchantment which is doomed to dramatic disintegration. Nevertheless, at the core of the play there is a cohesive thematic unity: the violation of conventional moral standards to achieve expressive freedom of love, a love so intense in its emotional demands that it borders on death. Against the backdrop of the denial of responsibility the conventional images of romantic love, as in her speech above, sound hollow and augment the play's effectual tragedy.

In the course of their flight, "he" and "she" have exchanged roles. At the outset she complained of the cold, but now it is he who complains. She has gained his warmth, and he now feels cold and lonely when exposed to the exigencies of their abortive passion, a passion devoid of the sense of security which he felt with his wife. Inadvertently and subconsciously the feeling of guilt and the sensation that they have evaded their responsibilities begin to invade their love. To nullify this sense of guilt they attempt to return to the pristine state of childhood innocence, and they pretend that they are brother and sister, a common enough motif in Branner's works. The intensity and finality of their mutual joy become so great that they border on the finality of death, and once again Branner indicates the relationship between love and death. They are related in the intensity of the emotions they evoke, for love is seen as the iterative death of losing one's self in another person. Possibility and reality have been fused together as the two lovers flee from London to Paris to Rome until, finally, the sense of guilt grows so strong that it necessitates the ultimate state of oneness wherein reality disappears:

No, I won't listen to them. Take me again, take me and be quiet. Bear me back to the dark where we are one—one flesh; where man and woman are the same, life and death the same, where there is no past and no future, and no voices—and no guilt—[22]

Their flight ends in Rome, where they hear the voices of the husband and wife they have abandoned. His wife has gone insane, and her husband has become paralyzed. Having heard their voices, she says that nothing can help them, for they are already dead. She says that they have dreamed the impossible—that it was possible to live without guilt, but now:

> And the guilt for their deaths—can that be loved away? That will follow us day and night. Until we become outlawed on earth and estranged from ourselves. . . . once dreamed about living without guilt. Now we know that that is impossible. We have looked back; we have turned from life to death. Now we must bear death and change it into life.[23]

The feeling of impending death has become so intense that it has been converted into a renewal of life, and they see things as if for the first time. Finally, at the conclusion of the play, they walk into the Protestant cemetery in Rome at Porta San Paolo. There they stand before Keats's and Shelley's graves and read the inscription: "Here lies one whose name was written upon the waters." By having chosen—without any genuinely open alternative—to live life and love each other, their lives have become something eternal, but with a meaning known only to themselves.

Et Spil om Kærligheden og Döden was Branner's first attempt at a dramatic tone poem, but the style he developed in that first attempt was to recur in *Mörket mellem Træerne* (1965),[24] his final radio play. This play is an almost uninterpretable pastiche of "he" and "she" voices which speak out without any reference to a consistent chronological or spatial pattern. It is as abstruse and abstract as *Finnegans Wake* and just as permissive of multiple interpretations. It is divided into four sections of unequal length: "Afternoon," "Evening," "Night," and "Morning," in which an author and his wife comment on their life together. The play's theme is the one central to Branner's later works that "one cannot flee from anything." This play is Branner's final statement that mutual love and understanding are prerequisites for individuation, for they are the only forces capable of alleviating loneliness.

Ariel (1963)[25] is Branner's last collection of short stories, and here he turns full circle back to the days of childhood and revokes one of the images from his earliest works: the child playing beside the shore. *Ariel* contains four longer stories which relate the conflict between the sexes.

In the first story, *Leg ved Stranden*, two children, Helle and

Andreas, retreat to a secret hole they have carved out between bushes beside the sea. There they realize that the innocent period together as childhood playmates has ended, for it is there that the new dimension of sexuality enters their lives. Helle and Andreas are Eva and Börge on the brink of puberty, and Helle contains all the features that we find in Katrine in *De blaa Undulater* and Eva in *Historien om Börge*. She is crafty, worldly wise and domineering. She has the same rigid exterior and delicately protected personal self as her predecessors. Andreas, like Börge, is the product of a severely religious home and he is dominated by Helle. He is, as Emil Frederiksen states:

. . . fixed in what the other stories also demonstrate: that the actual is incredible, impossible; it exists and yet it does not exist.[26]

As Helle and Andreas lie in their hut together, they become aware of each other as sexual beings, and they see their dependency on each other in a new light.

In the collection's title story, we meet a man as he awakens after having spent a night with his mistress. He rises early in the morning and leaves her in the cabin where they have spent the night. There is much that he wishes to say to her, but he cannot force himself to speak. The unsaid, he believes, is more pregnant with meaning than the said. Having left the cabin, he wanders through the fog until he finds a taxi and gets a ride back to his house. There he meets his crippled wife. In the bright morning light his anxiety and his guilt are met by the sight of a woman who feels that she has been miraculously cured while he was away. She utters not a word of reproach. The picture of her as a bright and ethereal being is contrasted with the dark vision of the illicit affair in the cabin. He breaks down and cries, and then feels himself borne through the air, like Ariel, "up into the high pure light of pain." [27]

The third story in the collection, *Puritanerne*, depicts the contrast between two brothers, Max Tode, a writer, and Godfred, a priest. Max is a mundane, wordly wise author who forms a direct contrast to his spiritual, puritanical brother, Godfred. Between them stands Mona, whom both have loved, each in his own way. To Godfred, Mona was a symbol of purity and virginity. To Max, she was but another in a long chain of women he had loved, and

Drama and Short Story once more

theirs had been a love–hate relationship in which he had thought of her as a child. Max visits Godfred in the hospital where he lies at death's door, infected by a psychosomatic illness. Godfred has always been ill, even as a child, and he and Max feel guilty for their father's death. In their last conversation together at the hospital, Godfred holds a philosophical monologue in which he explains many of the basic tenets of Branner's own philosophy of life. He says that to see the truth is to see one's responsibility. Godfred then expounds the course of his shifting conception of God:

> Now at length I know that it is impossible to approach God; it is vain to hope so, but I didn't know it then. I constantly made new pictures of false gods for myself. At first I tried to believe in an omnipotent paternal God who would judge me and punish me, and when I finally understood that all power stems from the devil, I sought an all-forgiving God who would take my guilt from me. But I couldn't place the burden of guilt on God either; I had to bear it myself if my life were to have meaning. Therefore, I created for myself a God beyond all humanity; a God who was always and all ways; but always and all ways is the same as never and nowhere—God's footsteps died away. His face became lost in formlessness, his name became a word without meaning. Finally it became clear to me that my wandering toward God had only led me farther and farther away from Him.[28]

Guilt and responsibility are once again stressed as having unequivocal priority above deity, and they are the epiphanies which blaze forth from Branner's best works. The quest of Godfred's self-mocking and self-tormenting consciousness has come to the perception of the concepts which give meaning to life and reality. It is a darkly pessimistic picture which emerges, but of guilt and responsibility are born the virtuous Christian ideals of service and selflessness, as they are for Clemens in *Rytteren* and Tomas in *Ingen kender Natten*. Godfred's name (God = "God" and *fred* = "peace") captures the bipolarity of his spiritual quest, and it is his refusal to accept aprioristic conceptualizations of a given philosophy and theology that has committed him to that quest. Initially, like Katrine in *De blaa Undulater,* he wanted a punitive response, for he wanted a God who would judge him and punish him, thereby alleviating him from accepting his guilt and responsibility. However, he has finally rejected the apotheosis of the "weak" person's God and, at death's door, Godfred has apprehended a vision of God which he can accept, for:

... now I am finally ready to go into the amorphous dark without hope and without fear. Perhaps it is the beginning of a belief in God.[29]

Godfred has ended with the same conception of God and realized the point at which faith begins in the same manner as Knud Mortimer in *Drömmen om en Kvinde,* and Branner has come full circle in his reasoned excursus on faith.

This story has none of the structural compactness and formal precision of Branner's earlier works. It is perhaps a final attempt to put his *Weltanschauung* into a definitive form, and it reads more like an *apologia* than an artistic creation.

The final story in the collection, *Skrevet i Vand,* evidences the same lyricism and the same disregard for formal clarity that we find in *Et Spil om Kærligheden og Döden* and *Mörket mellem Træerne.* It is perhaps the most fantastic and at the same time one of Branner's weakest short stories. It is divided into two parts. In the first part we meet an elderly couple on a plane as they are heading south for a holiday. During the flight he reflects on their life together. The second section of the story tells of their stay in Rome, where they glide apart and find each other again in all that they see. This story is an externalized piece of reflection upon reflection and has only slight confrontations with reality which allow the reader to fix upon recognizable points. Reality is but an inscription on the flood of time, and the reality of love is only obvious to those who experience it. It is something which loses its reality when it is communicated to someone else.

Epilogue

PREVIOUSLY we stated that Branner's works present a collage of attitudes, rather than a set of beliefs, and our review of his production—with emphasis placed on his earlier works—seems to support this view. The specific tone of Branner is that of a complex of moral attitudes: insistence on responsible social action as a moral and spiritual imperative, belief in the transformational power of love, acute awareness of the inadequacy of language in moments of creative desperation and the incompatibility of ethical and political realities. The techniques and patterns which Branner used and continually recreated and refined throughout his creative life seem admirably suited for a portrayal of these themes. In terms of creative evolution he moved away from the realism of the 1930s and finally embraced the plotless, psychological form evidenced by his last works. In this his career shows relatively the same technical movement as Strindberg's. Branner gradually emerged as a teller of tales of mythical proportions whose formal qualities coalesce with his overriding intellectual concern: to probe the depths of personality and reveal the hidden phenomena which lie behind its social masks. Branner's incessant experimentation may be ascribed to this concern. Nevertheless, despite the multiplicity of themes, genres, and approaches Branner attempted, a unity of imagery lies close beneath the surface of his multifaceted production, and this unified chain of images is constantly provided with a new contextual evaluation. We are continually confronted with the child's cry from the spiritual recesses of the adult. There is the clown figure who becomes ridiculous in his insistence on absolute goodness as he simultaneously exposes his moral frailty. There is the representative of nature as a morally blind force who directs the lives of others: Hans Egge and Hubert. There is the perpetual image of the archetypal woman in all her sensual splendor: Klara Kvistgaard, Birgitte

Böje, Merete Rude, Susanne, Irene, Lene, Helene, where the latter three are even nominally related. In the person of Lene this image achieves its symbolic zenith; as mother, sister, wife, and whore she is the woman of all men and the woman of no one man. There is the implementation of off-stage dying to confer the tonality of myth: *Eftermæle, Et Barn og en Mus, Historien om Börge, Drömmen en Kvinde, Rytteren, Söskende*.[1] The identification of God as a father figure is recurrent in *Historien om Börge, Rytteren,* and *Söskende*. The desire to flee from reality as a condition of psychic weakness is traceable as a theme from *Surdejgen* to *Skrevet i Vand* and is programmatically enunciated in *Samtale med en Klovn*. This form of weakness asserts itself as a demand for punishment to achieve security, a demand that is echoed in *Eftermæle, De blaa Undulater,* and *Skibet,* and one which is answered in the image of the punitive cellar in *Barnet leger ved Stranden, Rytteren,* and *Ingen kender Natten*. Thus, when viewed as a totality or individually, Branner's works reveal that he attempted depth and scope of characterization through the repetitive use of parallel scenes and key words and images, through inaudible thinking effectively verbalized as symbols or in the stream of consciousness, as in *Drömmen om en Kvinde* and *Ingen kender Natten*. The referential points for his repetitive suggestiveness are the polar opposites of good and evil and the psychic tensions they create, as Branner said:

> Man was driven from Paradise, and the concepts of good and evil came into the world in the form of an imperative question. That's what distinguishes Man from Nature, and no religious faith, no political dogma and no physical or psychic therapy can absolve the individual from making a decision about it.[2]

Many of Branner's themes and structural devices should be familiar to the student of American literature acquainted with John Updike, and Branner once professed deep admiration for Updike's work.[3] It is tantalizing to imagine how Branner would have received *Couples*, a work with obvious affinities to his own, had he lived.

Having followed Branner's development from his debut as a short story writer, we must conclude that he is, indeed, the author of life, death, and *angst*, a teller of tales of the child in man, and

Epilogue

one who insists on the acceptance of the humanistic imperative of communal responsibility if our lives are to have meaning. At the very heart of much of his writing stands the myth of death and spiritual rebirth through the agency of love. The road to death and rebirth is the route of maturation along which we have to accept certain ethical imperatives to define "life and reality." It is, as Branner himself said, the situations along that route which are interesting, and "it is the psychological impact of the situation which determines the individual."[4]

Notes and References

Chapter One

1. The two poplars are recurrent symbols in Branner's works. In addition to *Historien om Börge,* they are mentioned in *Glimt av mig selv, Surdejgen, Hannibals Træsko* and *Drömmen om en Kvinde.* According to C. J. Elmquist (*Politikens Kronik* 2/15/1950), they stand "like a portal at the entrance to his poetic world," and they probably also represent guardians at the gateway of childhood recollections.

2. First published in *Berlingske Aftenavis* (4/20/1940) and subsequently reprinted in *Profiler* (1944) and in Nordentoft's and Vosmar's *Röde heste i Sneen,* pp. 9–20, from which the quotations here are translated.

3. *Glimt av mig selv,* p. 9.

4. *Ibid.,* pp. 16–17.

5. Letter in Royal Library, Copenhagen.

6. The short stories are treated in chronological order through 1936, the year in which his first novel, *Legetöj,* appeared.

7. "Surdejgen," *Magasinet* (September 4, 1932). Nine days after the appearance of *Surdejgen,* Branner's first radio play, *Efterspil,* was broadcast. It has never been published.

8. *Magasinet* (December 4, 1932) and never subsequently republished.

9. Note the name, *Börner = börn-,* "children," a possible first example of Branner's use of name symbolism.

10. The lover who plays the role of a child and seeks a mother figure in the woman he loves is a recurring theme in Branner's works. For a list of occurrences, see Mogens Bröndsted, *Barnet hos H. C. Branner,* p. 129, fn. 11.

11. *Magasinet* (January 8, 1933) and republished in the anthology, *Om lidt er vi borte* (1939). Quotations are from the fifth edition (Copenhagen: Povl Branners Forlag, 1944), pp. 5–22.

12. *Magasinet* (July 2, 1933). This story has only its title, some names and the wife's death in common with the title story of the anthology, *To Minutters Stilhed* (1944). This earlier version has been

reprinted in *Gyldendals Julebog 1966,* pp. 7–24, from which the quotations here have been translated.
  13. *To Minutters Stilhed,* pp. 17–18.
  14. Of course, this is a common device in satire. Note, for example, how Sinclair Lewis employs it in *Main Street* to transform Carol Kennicott, an American Ragna, into a victim of tragic irony.
  15. Hans Scherfig, *Det forsömte Foraar* (Copenhagen: Gyldendal, 1940), p. 13.
  16. *To Minutters Stilhed,* pp. 24–25.
  17. Published in *Fem Radiospil,* pp. 7–50, from which the quotations here were translated.
  18. *Ibid.,* p. 21.
  19. Note that Claus Böje's son, Torkild, drowns himself in *Barnet leger ved Stranden* and that Claus also attempts to drown himself.
  20. Note the similarity in names: Claus Böje–Christian Boje.
  21. *Fem Radiospil,* p. 31.
  22. *Op. cit.,* p. 12.
  23. Interestingly enough, neither of these stories is listed by Vosmar, *H. C. Branner,* p. 177.
  24. *Magasinet* (February 4, 1934) and reprinted in *Gyldendals Julebog 1966,* pp. 26–40, from which the quotations here have been translated.
  25. *Magasinet* (April 29, 1934) and reprinted in the anthology, *Om lidt er vi borte,* pp. 23–39, with the title, *Et Barn og en Mus.* Quotations here were translated from the anthology.
  26. *Ibid.,* p. 23. Note that the seeds of the Garden of Eden myth which are planted here come to flower in *Historien om Börge,* see *infra,* p. 64 ff.
  27. *Ibid.,* p. 26.
  28. In *Tilbageblik paa 30' erne 2,* p. 122.
  29. *Et Barn og en Mus,* pp. 31–32.
  30. Cf. the analysis by Frederiksen, *H. C. Branner,* pp. 33–34.
  31. *Magasinet* (September 2, 1934) and republished in *Nye Danske Noveller* (1945). Quotations here were translated from *Magasinet.*
  32. Vosmar, *H. C. Branner,* p. 75.
  33. *Gyldendals Julebog 1966,* pp. 41–49.
  34. *Ibid.,* p. 49.
  35. "Hvad er Sandhed?" (*Magasinet* February 3, 1935) has never been republished and was not available to me.
  36. *Magasinet* (July 21, 1935) and reprinted in *Om lidt er vi borte,* pp. 61–83.
  37. *Magasinet* (January 12, 1936) and reprinted in *Om lidt er vi borte,* pp. 84–103, from which the quotations here have been translated.

Notes and References

38. *Ibid.*, p. 92.
39. *Tilbageblik paa 30' erne* 2, p. 126.
40. *Magasinet* (March 1, 1936) and not subsequently reprinted.
41. *Magasinet* (July 19, 1936) and reprinted in *Om lidt er vi borte*, pp. 104–125.
42. *Hvad er Sandhed?* is the only story omitted from the survey.
43. Personal interview with H. C. Branner, September 7, 1965.
44. *Dæmoner ved Daggry* in *Vandring langs Floden*, pp. 146–47.
45. Cf. Mogens Bröndsted, *Barnet hos H. C. Branner*.
46. *Ibid.*, p. 128 ff., and Vosmar, *H. C. Branner*, pp. 23–29.
47. *Politiken* (November 23, 1941).
48. Letter from H. C. Branner to Holger Kristiansen (July 3, 1937), Royal Library, Copenhagen. At the time Kristiansen was an unemployed worker who had formed a reading circle for other unemployed workers. One of the novels discussed by the group was *Legetöj*. Uncertain of their interpretation, Kristiansen wrote to Branner and asked him what his intention had been. Sympathetic to the workers and flattered that they had selected his novel, Branner replied with one of the most ingenuous commentaries on his works he ever made.
49. *Tilbageblik paa 30' erne* 2, p. 8.
50. The contrast between, for example, Herman Kejser's idealized view of himself as a Napoleonic commander and Herman Kejser as he really is—an impotent, vacillating character incapable of directing the course of his life.
51. Note that Branner often uses Herman to designate an ineffectual character, as Herman in *Eftermæle*, *To Minutters Stilhed* and *Tre Mænd vender hjem*.
52. *Legetöj*, 5th. ed. (Copenhagen: Gyldendal, 1961), p. 287.
53. Vosmar, *H. C. Branner*, p. 24.
54. *Ibid.*, pp. 12, 14, 15, 18, 21, 32, 37, 72, 73, 90, 109, 111, 114, 116, 118, 138, 145, 156, 158, 201, 223, 246, 247, 283, 299, 313, 315.
55. Note the possibility of autobiographical reference, as Branner says that he pretended that his bike was a horse in *Dæmoner ved Daggry*, p. 151.
56. Branner often refers to the captain of industry as a Napoleonic figure, as in *To Minutters Stilhed*, *Isaksen* and *Tre Mænd vender hjem*. This reference may derive from Jacob Paludan's *Jörgen Stein* (1932–1933), where Torvald, a symbol of the old order, is characterized as a Napoleon figure as he directs WW I on a map in his provincial study. The influence of this monumental Danish novel cannot be overestimated.
57. Of course, there are many variations and combinations of the character types outlined here, and some more readily fall into the established categories than others. For example, Clemens in *Rytteren*

is a clown type, but definitely incapable of dominating others. On the matter of character types in Branner's works, see Vosmar, *H. C. Branner*, pp. 13–29.

58. Cf. Petra in Jörgen Nielsen's short story, *Möbel-Psykose*. A literary ancestor is Mrs. Gereth in Henry James's *The Spoils of Poynton*.

59. This device was first used by Branner in *Eftermæle*, where the characters were revealed by their reactions to the central incident of Cæcilie Hermansen's death. It is found again in *Drömmen om en Kvinde* in the parallel cathedral scenes, see *infra*, p. 54 ff.

60. *Legetöj*, p. 86.
61. *Ibid.*, p. 164.
62. *Ibid.*, p. 79.

Chapter Two

1. Vosmar, *H. C. Branner*, p. 48.
2. Claus Böje's restrictive attitude toward the boy is doubtless the result of a complex caused by his own puritanical childhood. To avenge the way his father had treated him, he represses the child, who then has only his mother as a source of affection and understanding. Bewildered and reprimanded at every turn by his father, Torkild sees death as the only escape. From the evidence given in the novel this seems a more plausible explanation of Torkild's suicide than that given by P. M. Mitchell in his *A History of Danish Literature* (Copenhagen: Gyldendal, 1957), p. 270, where he states that: "It is fear of life and fear of unknown forces which drive the child to his death. . . .".
3. *Barnet leger ved Stranden*, p. 175.
4. *Ibid.*, pp. 188–89.
5. *Ibid.*, p. 189.
6. *Ibid.*, p. 279.
7. See *infra*, p. 132.
8. *Barnet leger ved Stranden*, p. 30.
9. *Ibid.*, p. 75.
10. *Ibid.*, p. 155 and cf. Fonsmark, *H. C. Branner*, p. 16.
11. *Ibid.*, p. 143.
12. Cf. Mogens Bröndsted, *Barnet hos H. C. Branner*, pp. 131–32 and see *Barnet leger ved Stranden*, p. 142.
13. *Barnet leger ved Stranden*, pp. 110, 111, 112.
14. *Ibid.*, p. 204.
15. *Ibid.*, p. 279.
16. In *Vandring langs Floden*, p. 49.
17. Mogens Bröndsted, *Barnet hos H. C. Branner*, p. 131 ff. and cf. Vosmar, *H. C. Branner*, p. 55.
18. Bröndsted, *loc. cit.*

Notes and References

19. See Konstantin Reichardt, *Tragedy of Idealism: Henrik Ibsen* in *Tragic Themes in Western Literature*. Ed. by Cleanth Brooks (New Haven: Yale University Press, 1955), p. 139.
20. *Glimt av mig selv*, p. 20.
21. Vosmar, *H. C. Branner*, p. 56.
22. *Ibid.*, p. 57.
23. The analytical detachment evidenced by passages such as those cited above (*supra*, p. 40) is not in keeping with a person who supposedly lacks this very quality.
24. Frederiksen, *H. C. Branner*, p. 26.
25. *Ibid.*, p. 28.
26. Letter to Holger Kristiansen (July 3, 1937).
27. Paul la Cour, "Freud og Litteraturen," *Tilskueren* 49. 25–34 (1932).
28. *Ibid.*, p. 31.
29. *Ibid.*, p. 32.
30. *Ibid.*, p. 33.
31. "Dr. Næsgaard og Psykoanalysen," *Ekstrabladets Kronik* (October 27, 1933) and reprinted in Kai Friis Möller, *Et Narreskib* (Copenhagen: Miloske Bogtrykkeris Forlag, 1935), pp. 19–25, from which the quotations here have been translated.
32. Sigurd Næsgaard, *Psykoanalyse* 1–2 (Copenhagen: Funkis Forlag, 1933).
33. *Barnet leger ved Stranden*, p. 187.
34. *Ibid.*, p. 188.
35. *Ibid.*, pp. 11, 29, 30, 42, 72, 95, 200.
36. Quotations here were, except where indicated otherwise, translated from the abridged edition (Copenhagen: Gyldendal, 1956). Only the first edition (Copenhagen: Povl Branner, 1941) is unabridged.
37. *Politiken* (November 23, 1941).
38. *Drömmen om en Kvinde*, pp. 236–37.
39. *Ibid.*, pp. 67–68.
40. Cf. Vosmar, *H. C. Branner*, p. 65.
41. *Drömmen om en Kvinde*, p. 220.
42. *Ibid.*, pp. 221–22.
43. *Ibid.*, pp. 148, 228.
44. *Ibid.*, p. 223.
45. Finally, note the repeated use of hand symbols, *ibid.*, pp. 9, 10, 13, 14, 15, 22, 26, 28, 39, 41, 42, 46, 48, 49, 69, 79, 92, 93, 95, 133, 147, 148, 162, 168, 170, 171, 172, 176, 179, 191, 194, 198, 200, 202, 212, 220, 223, 224, 225, 228, 239.
46. *Ibid.*, p. 277.
47. Mogens Bröndsted and Sven Möller Kristensen, *Danmarks Litteratur* (Copenhagen: Gyldendal, 1963), p. 295.

48. *Drömmen om en Kvinde,* p. 23.
49. *Ibid.,* p. 40 ff.
50. *Ibid.,* pp. 42–49 and does not occur again until p. 127.
51. *Ibid.,* p. 127.
52. *Ibid.,* p. 207.
53. Branner is here re-using an image first employed in the short story *Om lidt er vi borte* (1939), p. 193, in which the wandering observer pauses outside a window to note the fish-like faces of those who live inside.
54. E.g., *ibid.,* pp. 11, 23, 25, 55, 58, 60, 69, 70, 76, 143, 145, 147, 148, 153, 173, 256.
55. *Drömmen om en Kvinde* (1941), p. 66.
56. *Ibid.,* p. 76.
57. *Ibid.,* pp. 76–77.
58. Ernest Hemingway, *For Whom the Bell Tolls* (New York: Charles Scribner's Sons, 1955), p. 159.
59. Personal interview with H. C. Branner, September 7, 1965.
60. *Drömmen om en Kvinde* (1941), p. 87.
61. *Barnet leger ved Stranden,* p. 279.
62. *Drömmen om en Kvinde* (1941), pp. 153–54.
63. Frederiksen, *H. C. Branner,* p. 52.
64. "Et grædende Barn" in *Vandring langs Floden,* pp. 57–58.
65. *Drömmen om en Kvinde,* p. 133.
66. It is unknown to what extent Branner read or was influenced by Jung. Nevertheless, here and elsewhere reference to Jung does not necessarily mean that Branner consciously drew upon Jung's ideas nor that Branner's works may be fitted into strictly Jungian patterns. Moreover, it should be noted that Jung first came into vogue in Danish literary circles after World War II.
67. Quotations are translated from the fourth edition (Copenhagen: Gyldendal, 1965). The first edition was published by Povl Branner, Copenhagen, 1942.
68. Vosmar, *H. C. Branner,* pp. 77–80.
69. Personal interview with H. C. Branner, September 7, 1965.
70. *Historien om Börge,* p. 23.
71. *Ibid.,* p. 33.
72. *Ibid.,* p. 36.
73. *Ibid.,* p. 47 and cf. pp. 52–53.
74. *Ibid.,* p. 59.
75. *Ibid.,* pp. 22, 44, 48, 57, 93, 154, 181, 185.
76. *Glimt av mig selv,* p. 10.
77. *Historien om Börge,* p. 56.
78. *Ibid.,* p. 56. Note that the desire to curl oneself up and hide from reality at a time of crisis is a common feature in many of Bran-

Notes and References

ner's works and is perhaps an autobiographical reference. We find a clear instance of this posture in *Barnet leger ved Stranden*, where, at the conclusion of the novel, Claus Böje attempts to hide in the potato pit, see Mogens Bröndsted, *Barnet hos H. C. Branner*, p. 118. A prominent recurrence of this image is when Simon hides in the cellar prior to his confrontation with Tomas in *Ingen kender Natten*. That the reference may be autobiographical is indicated by Branner's description of how he himself tried to hide in the autobiographical *Dæmoner ved Daggry* in *Vandring langs Floden*, p. 152: "I sat there with my knees drawn up under me and my face hidden in my hands just like when I was a little boy. I usually cried a little, then I would begin to laugh and sing in a high, unnatural voice and toward morning I would make up poems."

79. *Historien om Börge*, p. 50.
80. *Ibid.*, p. 67.
81. *Ibid.*, p. 34.
82. *Ibid.*, pp. 72–73.
83. Cf. *supra*, p. 21 Börge's reaction to death in *Et Barn og en Mus*.
84. *Historien om Börge*, p. 75.
85. *Ibid.*, pp. 83–84.
86. *Ibid.*, p. 103.
87. *Ibid.*, p. 112.
88. *Historien om Börge*, p. 138.
89. *Ibid.*, p. 168.
90. *Ibid.*, p. 195.

Chapter Three

1. (Copenhagen: Povl Branners Forlag, 1939). Quotations here were taken from the fifth edition (1944).
2. Hans Hertel in *Tilbageblik paa 30' erne* 1, pp. 20–21.
3. This story had appeared with the title, *Boheme*, in *Hjemmets Söndag* (May 7, 1939).
4. *To Minutters Stilhed* (Copenhagen: Povl Branners Forlag, 1944).
5. *Politiken* (October 3, 1939).
6. *Ibid., loc. cit.*
7. First published in *Magasinet* (October 16, 1938) and subsequently in *Om lidt er vi borte*, pp. 126–146.
8. First published in *Hjemmets Söndag* (April 16, 1939) and subsequently in *Om lidt er vi borte*, pp. 147–67.
9. *Om lidt er vi borte*, p. 158.
10. *Ibid.*, p. 167.
11. First published in *Magasinet* (July 4, 1939) and subsequently reprinted in *Om lidt er vi borte*, pp. 168–87, from which the quotations here have been translated.

12. *Om lidt er vi borte,* pp. 188–208.
13. *Ibid.,* pp. 207–208.
14. *Ibid.,* p. 208.
15. Emil Aarestrup, *Samlede Verker.* Ed. by Hans Brix and Palle Rævnkjær. Vol. 3 (Copenhagen: Henrik Koppels Forlag, 1923), p. 221.
16. *Skibet* was first published in *Berlingske Tidende*'s Sunday Supplement (October 20, 1940) and subsequently reprinted in *To Minutters Stilhed,* pp. 7–34, from which the quotations here have been translated.
17. *Ibid.,* p. 29.
18. Johan Borgen, "Profilen: H. C. Branner," *Vinduet* 16 (1962), p. 172.
19. First published in *Jul i Danmark* (1943) and subsequently in *To Minutters Stilhed,* pp. 35–36.
20. First published in *Magasinet* (April 17, 1938) and subsequently in *To Minutters Stilhed,* pp. 57–81.
21. First published in *Berlingske Tidende*'s Sunday Supplement (November 19, 1939) and subsequently reprinted in *To Minutters Stilhed,* pp. 82–103, from which the quotation here has been translated.
22. *Ibid.,* p. 102.
23. First published in *Berlinkske Tidende*'s Sunday Supplement (October 5, 1941) and subsequently reprinted in *To Minutters Stilhed,* pp. 104–20.
24. Personal interview with H. C. Branner, September 7, 1965.
25. First published in *To Minutters Stilhed,* pp. 121–45.
26. *Ibid.,* p. 143.
27. First published in *Berlingske Tidende*'s Sunday Supplement (October 1, 1939) and subsequently reprinted in *To Minutters Stilhed,* pp. 146–66.
28. Frederiksen, *H. C. Branner,* pp. 68–69.
29. *Om lidt er vi borte,* p. 155.
30. First published in *To Minutters Stilhed,* pp. 167–96.
31. Vosmar, *H. C. Branner,* p. 74.
32. *To Minutters Stilhed,* p. 195.
33. First published in *Hjemmets Söndag* (April 30, 1944) and subsequently reprinted in *To Minutters Stilhed,* pp. 197–213, from which the quotation here has been translated.
34. *Ibid.,* p. 213.
35. First published in *Arbejdernes Almanak* (1943) and subsequently reprinted in *To Minutters Stilhed,* pp. 214–32, from which the quotation here has been translated.
36. *Ibid.,* p. 232.

Notes and References

37. First published in *Vandring langs Floden,* pp. 33–43.
38. First published with the title, *Boheme,* in *Hjemmets Söndag* (May 7, 1939) and subsequently reprinted with this title in *30 Danske Noveller,* pp. 9–21, from which the quotation here was taken.
39. *Magasinet* (January 29, 1939) and not subsequently reprinted.
40. This story was not available to me. It was first published in *Hjemmet* Nr. 28 (1939) and subsequently republished in *Politikens Nu* (February 15, 1955).
41. (Copenhagen: Carit Andersens Forlag, 1946) and republished in *Vandring langs Floden,* pp. 9–29.
42. First broadcast (February 19, 1937) and, interestingly enough, probably written while Branner was still at work on *Barnet leger ved Stranden* with which it shows a certain affinity. It was later published in *Fem Hörespil* (1943) and subsequently republished in *Fem Radiospil* (Copenhagen: Gyldendal, 1965), pp. 51–93, from which the quotations here have been translated.
43. *Ibid.,* p. 60.
44. *Ibid.,* p. 73.
45. *Ibid.,* p. 74.
46. *Ibid.,* p. 79.
47. *Ibid.,* pp. 86–87.
48. *Paradokset Kjeld Abell* in *En bog om Kjeld Abell.* Ed. by Sven Möller Kristensen (Copenhagen: Gyldendal, 1961), pp. 162–65.

Chapter Four

1. Subsequently reprinted in *Gyldendals Julebog 1966,* pp. 50–75, from which the quotations here have been translated.
2. Johan Borgen, "Profilen: H. C. Branner," *Vinduet* 16 (1962), p. 173.
3. Frederiksen, *H. C. Branner,* p. 78.
4. *Trommerne,* p. 66.
5. *Brev til Johan* in *Johan Borgen* (Oslo: Oslo University Press, 1962), p. 17.
6. *Trommerne,* p. 54.
7. *Ibid.,* p. 75.
8. Note that *Barnet leger ved Stranden* (p. 279), *Dæmoner ved Daggry* (p. 161) and *Ingen kender Natten* (pp. 312–13) all conclude with a vision of hope. This vision is most effectively presented in *Ingen kender Natten,* where Tomas, the lone survivor in a warehouse, momentarily catches a glimpse of Frelserkirken at dawn with its figure of Christ, and the novel closes with his last hopeful thought: "eternally now shines the light of life."
9. First published in the illegal anthology *Der brænder en Ild* (1944), and subsequently published together with *Bjergene* (Copen-

hagen: Gyldendal, 1953) from which the quotations here have been translated.
10. *Angst*, p. 68.
11. *Ibid.*, p. 15.
12. *Ibid.*, p. 21.
13. *Trommerne*, p. 50.
14. *Angst*, p. 9.
15. Vosmar, *H. C. Branner*, p. 89.
16. Although originally conceived as a short story, *Rytteren* was expanded into a novella and a play, both of which were completed in the same year. The novella was first published on December 8, 1949, while the text of the drama was not published until 1968 (*Tre Skuespil*, Copenhagen: Gyldendal, 1968) from which the quotation here has been translated. The text of the play is found in two versions. One, undoubtedly the original version from 1949, is quite long, while the other published version, a greatly revised and abridged text, was used for the performance at Copenhagen's Det nye Teater, February 12, 1952, when the play had its Danish premiere. The novella was first published by Branner og Korchs Forlag, Copenhagen, 1949. The quotations here have been translated from the ninth edition (Copenhagen: Gyldendal, 1964).
17. *Politiken* (December 8, 1949).
18. *Berlingske Tidende* (December 8, 1949).
19. Cf. *infra*, fn. 21.
20. Niels Kaas Johansen, "Rytteren i ny belysning," *Gads Danske Magasin* 24. 97–102 (1950).
21. H. C. Branner, *Nationaltidende* (December 18, 1949).
22. "'Rytteren' belyst af en almindelig Læser," *Berlingske Aftenavis*'s Kronik (February 21, 1950).
23. Thorkild Björnvig, *Kains Alter: Martin A. Hansens Digtning og Tænkning* (Copenhagen: Gyldendal, 1964), p. 547.
24. Cf. Steen Eiler Rasmussen, "Karen Blixens Rungstedlund" in *Det Danske Akademi 1960–1967* (Copenhagen: G. E. C. Gads Forlag, 1967), pp. 290, 292.
25. *Rytteren*, p. 52.
26. H. C. Branner: "Rytteren," *Bazar* 1–2, 51–63, 71–94 (1957) and subsequently republished in *Essays* (Copenhagen: Gyldendal, 1965), pp. 185–220, to which the references here are made.
27. *Karen Blixens Rungstedlund*, pp. 274–90.
28. *Spögelseshestene* (Copenhagen: Forlaget Fremad, 1955).
29. *Karen Blixens Rungstedlund*, pp. 285–86.
30. H. C. Branner: "Rytteren," p. 216.
31. *Ibid.*, p. 203.
32. *Rytteren* (play), p. 41. "SUSANNE: Herman? . . . . Susanne.

Notes and References

Don't you even recognize my voice? All your horses probably still do, although it's been a whole. . . ." A *whole* is in the neuter which can only refer to the neuter *ar*, "year."

33. Frederiksen, *H. C. Branner*, p. 85.
34. Vosmar, *H. C. Branner*, p. 97.
35. *Rytteren*, p. 155.
36. Vosmar, *H. C. Branner*, p. 107.
37. *Rytteren*, p. 47.
38. *Ibid.*, pp. 51–52.
39. Cf. Karen Blixen, *H. C. Branner: "Rytteren,"* p. 211.
40. *Rytteren*, p. 152.
41. *Rytteren*, Act. IV:2, p. 74.
42. *Rytteren*, pp. 39, 40, 41, 76, 77, 92, 96, 116, 121, 137.
43. Vosmar, *H. C. Branner*, p. 101.
44. *Politiken* (January 4, 1952).
45. *Politiken*'s Kronik (1/1/1950) and subsequently republished in *Vandring langs Floden*, pp. 95–107.
46. *Politiken* (January 4, 1952).
47. (Copenhagen: Gyldendal, 1952) and subsequently republished in *Tre Skuespil*, pp. 81–151, from which the quotations here have been translated.
48. *Ibid.*, p. 104.
49. *Ibid.*, p. 105.
50. *Ibid.*, p. 112.
51. *Ibid.*, p. 129.
52. *Ibid.*, p. 131.
53. *Ibid.*, p. 148.
54. "Omkring et skuespil," *Politiken*'s Kronik (March 2, 1952).
55. Vosmar, *H. C. Branner*, p. 120.
56. *Ibid.*, p. 122. Note the reference to the Pauline doctrine of the Anti-Christ, Second Thessalonians 2:3–9.

Chapter Five

1. (Copenhagen: Gyldendal, 1953) which also contains *Angst*, first published separately as *Boghallens Julegave* in 1947.
2. *Bjergene*, pp. 82–83.
3. *Ibid.*, p. 83.
4. Vosmar, *H. C. Branner*, p. 126.
5. *Bjergene*, p. 157.
6. Frederiksen, *H. C. Branner*, p. 82.
7. *Bjergene*, pp. 160–61.
8. *Döden varer saa længe* (*Vandring langs Floden*, pp. 61–77) was written in 1947 and tells of an author who makes a tour to postwar Germany to lecture on *Die Krise des Humanismus*.

9. *Digteren og pigen* in *Vandring langs Floden*, pp. 9–29.
10. *Ibid.*, p. 9.
11. *Ibid.*, p. 19.
12. Note, however, that the terms of Kierkegaardian thought are found in *Bjergene*, as, for example, p. 166: "for that was the paradox, that was the truth."
13. Interview with H. C. Branner, September 7, 1965.
14. Branner lectured in Germany on *Die Krise des Humanismus* shortly after the war.
15. Branner translated *The Trial* in 1945 and *The Castle* in 1949.
16. Georg Lukács, *The Meaning of Contemporary Realism* trans. by John and Necke Mander (London: Merlin Press, 1963), p. 36.
17. Frederiksen, *H. C. Branner*, p. 82.
18. *Bjergene*, p. 168.
19. *Ibid.*, p. 161.
20. Vosmar, *H. C. Branner*, p. 125.
21. *Angst*, Boghallens Julegave (Copenhagen: Nordlundes Bog-
22. Tom Kristensen, "To Tidsbilleder af H. C. Branner," *Essayer* (Copenhagen: Gyldendal, 1967), p. 136.
23. *Vandring langs Floden*, p. 129.
24. *Ibid.*, p. 116.
25. Personal interview with Tarjei Vesaas, July 5, 1965.
26. Personal interview with H. C. Branner, September 7, 1965.
27. Frederiksen, *H. C. Branner*, p. 105.
28. Henrik Ibsen, "Brændte Skibe" (1871) in *Samlede Verker*, Vol. 14 (Oslo: Gyldendal norsk forlag, 1937), p. 433. My translation.
29. H. C. Branner, "Fragment af novellen, *Ingen kender Natten*," *Ord och Bild* 61, 80–82 (1952). This fragment corresponds to *Ingen kender Natten* (Copenhagen: Gyldendal, 1955), pp. 9–13. Only the final sections of the fragment are altered in the novel version, and the alterations appear to be quite minor. Cf., for example: "life and blood and everything came out of him and that was to die, that was first to die." (frag., p. 82) vs. "life and blood and everything came out of him, and he looked down at it in horror, for that was just like watching himself die." (novel, p. 13).
30. See Mogens Bröndsted, *Barnet hos H. C. Branner*, p. 155.
31. Sven Möller Kristensen, "H. C. Branner: *Ingen kender Natten*" in *Digtning og livssyn* (Copenhagen: Gyldendal, 1960), p. 199. This is the most thorough analysis of the novel to date and contains many excellent observations.
32. Cf. similar scenes in *Barnet leger ved Stranden* (p. 279); the cathedral scenes in *Drömmen om en Kvinde* (pp. 221–22, 227); *Trommerne* (p. 75); *Angst* (p. 68); *Dæmoner ved Daggry* (p. 161),

where, as in *Ingen kender Natten* (p. 313), the tones of *Den signede Dag* are also heard from Frelserkirken.

33. Cf. Vosmar, *H. C. Branner*, p. 147, and note, for example, the play of light and dark in Gabriel's villa (p. 105) and in "Night" in *Rytteren* (pp. 169–79), where Clemens wanders in and out of the light. In his review of *Ingen kender Natten* Tom Kristensen stated: "The flight is excitingly told, for Branner's fantasy works best with dark and glaring light effects." (*Politiken*, December 5, 1955.)

34. *Ingen kender Natten*, pp. 9–13.

35. Cf. Katrine vs. Börge in *De blaa Undulater*, Eva vs. Börge in *Historien om Börge* and the affect of the unnamed playmate on Branner himself in *Glimt af mig selv*.

36. *Ingen kender Natten*, p. 13, cf. p. 22. Feddersen in *Legetöj* was also placed in a cellar, as was Claus Böje in *Barnet leger ved Stranden* (p. 11, cf. pp. 29, 30, 42, 72, 95, 200) and Clemens in *Rytteren* (p. 55).

37. Note that Tomas, whose mother has prostituted herself, and Lydia share a common trait of immobility. Hers is, to be sure, social, while his is physical.

38. *Ingen kender Natten*, p. 106.

39. *Ibid.*, p. 59.

40. *Ibid.*, p. 21.

41. *Ibid.*, p. 29.

42. *Ibid.*, p. 30.

43. *Ibid.*, p. 31.

44. Note that Winnie, Claus's wife in *Bjergene*, continually mocked him by calling him "clumsy Claus."

45. *Ingen kender Natten*, p. 32.

46. Guilt for imagining oneself as the agent of a person's death is, of course, a common theme in Branner's works. Claus in *Bjergene* (p. 121) feels guilty for having caused a cripple's death. Clemens in *Rytteren* feels guilty for having caused his mother's death. Michael in *Söskende* feels guilty for having caused a woman's death.

47. Cf. Katrine's attitude toward her parakeets in *De blaa Undulater* when she learns that her father believes she cares for them.

48. *Ingen kender Natten*, p. 39.

49. *Ibid.*, p. 37.

50. *Ibid.*, p. 31 and cf. Vosmar, *H. C. Branner*, p. 132.

51. *Ingen kender Natten*, pp. 42–43.

52. *Ibid.*, p. 45.

53. *Ibid.*, p. 53.

54. Jörn Vosmar, "Barnet leger ved Stranden," *Politiken*'s Kronik (March 21, 1956).

55. *Ingen kender Natten*, p. 185.
56. Cf. *Bjergene*, p. 110 and *Ingen kender Natten*, pp. 204–205.
57. *Ingen kender Natten*, pp. 60–70.
58. *Ibid.*, p. 65.
59. *Ibid.*, p. 168.
60. *Ibid.*, pp. 71–120.
61. *Ibid.*, p. 72.
62. *Ibid.*, p. 74.
63. *Ibid.*, pp. 78, 85.
64. *Ibid.*, p. 78. The use of reiterative melody to describe Felix's ritualistic sex acts suggests the inevitability of fate. Cf. the use of the same image in *Jeg ved en Fuglerede* (1948) (*Vandring langs Floden*, p. 83): "The needle went round and round in the same groove: Lust of the flesh and the soul's incurable loneliness, lust of the flesh and the soul's incurable loneliness, lust of the flesh and the soul's incurable loneliness. . . ." Branner rarely made literary allusions, and *Ingen kender Natten* provides the highest number of occurrences. This image is actually an allusion to Hjalmar Söderberg's *Gertrud* which has the motto: "The only thing I believe in is the lust of the flesh and the soul's incurable loneliness" on the title page.
65. *Ibid.*, p. 81.
66. *Ibid.*, pp. 106–107.
67. *Ibid.*, pp. 122–80.
68. Tomas had first met Gabriel on a boat from Antwerp before the war. Cf. *Sidste Skib*, pp. 37–38.
69. Cf. Vosmar, *H. C. Branner*, p. 134.
70. *Ingen kender Natten*, p. 162.
71. *Ibid.*, p. 167.
72. *Ibid.*, p. 169.
73. *Ibid.*, p. 166. This is a repeated refrain: pp. 25, 28, 157, 218, 263, 265.
74. *Ibid.*, p. 174.
75. Note that Irene performs the same act in a similar situation in *Söskende*.
76. *Ingen kender Natten*, p. 175.
77. Cf. the use of the child's cry motif in Branner's earlier works: *Barnet leger ved Stranden* (p. 279), *Drömmen om en Kvinde* (pp. 153–55), as well as elsewhere in *Ingen kender Natten* (p. 215, cf. pp. 219, 221) and see Vosmar, *H. C. Branner*, p. 148.
78. *Ingen kender Natten*, pp. 183–222.
79. *Ibid.*, p. 208.
80. *Ibid.*, p. 210.
81. *Ibid.*, p. 232, cf. p. 233.
82. *Ibid.*, p. 292.

Notes and References

83. Cf. Sven Möller Kristensen, *Digtning og livssyn*, p. 196.
84. *Ingen kender Natten*, p. 292 and cf. *Drömmen om en Kvinde*, p. 74 ff., where practically the same phraseology is used in a similar reincarnation scene.
85. Cf., for example, the effect Lene has on Tomas with the effect Kari has on the Saint in Sigurd Hoel's *Möte ved milepelen* (1947) (Oslo: Gyldendal norsk forlag, 1954), p. 245.

Chapter Six

1. *Vandring langs Floden* contains: *Digteren og Pigen* (1945), *Sidste Skib* (1939), *Et grædende Barn* (1946), *Döden varer saa længe* (1947), *Jeg ved en Fuglerede* (1948), *Samtale med en Klovn* (1950), *Vandring langs Floden* (1952) and *Dæmoner ved Daggry* (1956).
2. Frederiksen, *H. C. Branner*, pp. 115–16.
3. *Vandring langs Floden*, p. 51. Although supposedly written in 1946, this essay first appeared in *Magasinet* (February 4, 1956), the first part of which appears in *Vandring langs Floden*, pp. 47–58, while the second part appears in the same collection in a thoroughly revised version as *Dæmoner ved Daggry*, pp. 135–62.
4. *Vandring langs Floden*, p. 52.
5. *Syner og hvirvel* (Copenhagen: Gyldendal, 1965), p. 113.
6. *Kunstens Uafhængighed*, *Politiken*'s Kronik (November 25, 1956) and Copenhagen: Gyldendal, 1957, from which the quotations here have been translated.
7. *Kunstens Uafhængighed*, p. 5.
8. In answer to the question: "What do you do when you can't find yourself?" in an interview in *Politiken* (December 18, 1949), Branner replied: "Search."
9. *Kunstens Uafhængighed*, p. 22.
10. *Ibid.*, p. 11.
11. *Ibid.*, p. 8.
12. First broadcast (October 16, 1956) and filmed shortly thereafter by Nordisk Film. It was then published in *Fem Radiospil*, pp. 161–235.
13. *Thermopylæ* was first published in the same year (Copenhagen: Gyldendal, 1958) and subsequently republished in *Tre Skuespil*, pp. 155–263, from which the quotation here has been translated.
14. Cf. Vosmar, *H. C. Branner*, p. 158.
15. *Thermopylæ*, p. 245.
16. Subsequently printed in *Politiken*'s Kronik (January 4, 1959) and included in the collection, *Sidst i August*, pp. 162–68, from which the quotations here have been translated.
17. *Et Nytårsklokke*, p. 164.

18. *Ibid.*, p. 165.
19. *Ibid.*, p. 168.
20. *Et Spil om Kærligheden og Döden* (Copenhagen: Gyldendal, 1960) from which the quotations here have been translated.
21. *Ibid.*, p. 47.
22. *Ibid.*, p. 123.
23. *Ibid.*, p. 135.
24. First published in *Fem Radiospil*, pp. 239-82.
25. (Copenhagen: Gyldendal, 1964) from which the quotations here have been translated.
26. Frederiksen, *H. C. Branner*, p. 133.
27. *Ariel*, p. 64.
28. *Ibid.*, pp. 109-10.
29. *Ibid.*, p. 111.

Epilogue

1. See Richard B. Vowles, "Bergman, Branner and Off-Stage Dying." *Scandinavian Studies* 33, 1-9 (1961).
2. *Politiken* (January 4, 1959).
3. Personal interview with H. C. Branner, September 7, 1965.
4. *Ibid.*

Selected Bibliography

WORKS BY BRANNER

"Surdejgen," *Magasinet*. September 4, 1932.
"Prometheus," *Magasinet*. December 4, 1932.
"Drömmeren," *Magasinet*. October 1, 1933.
"Bogholder Mortensen og Greta Garbo," *Magasinet*. September 2, 1934.
"Tre mænd vender hjem," *Magasinet*. July 19, 1936.
Legetöj. (1936) 5th ed. Copenhagen: Gyldendal, 1961.
Barnet leger ved Stranden. Copenhagen: Povl Branner, 1937.
"Grænselandet," *Magasinet*. April 16, 1939.
Om lidt er vi borte. (1939) 5th ed. Copenhagen: Povl Branner, 1944.
Drömmen om en Kvinde. Copenhagen: Povl Branner, 1941, 3rd. rev. ed. Copenhagen: Gyldendal, 1967.
Historien om Börge. (1942) 4th impression. Copenhagen: Gyldendal, 1965.
To Minutters Stilhed. Copenhagen: Povl Branner, 1944.
Rytteren. Copenhagen: Branner og Korch, 1949.
Humanismens Krise. Mennesket i Tiden, Vol. I. Copenhagen: Hans Reitzels Forlag, 1950.
Söskende. Copenhagen: Branner og Korch, 1952.
Bjergene. Copenhagen: Gyldendal, 1953.
Ingen kender Natten. Copenhagen: Gyldendal, 1955.
Vandring langs Floden. Copenhagen: Gyldendal, 1956.
Kunstens Uafhængighed. Copenhagen: Gyldendal, 1957.
Thermopylæ. Copenhagen: Gyldendal, 1958.
Et Spil om Kærligheden og Döden. Copenhagen: Gyldendal, 1960.
"En Nytårsklokke." *Sidst i August: Et H. C. Branner-udvalg*. Ed. by L. Nordentoft and J. Vosmar. Copenhagen: Gyldendal, 1962.
"Glimt af mig selv." *Röde Heste i Sneen: Et H. C. Branner-udvalg*. Ed. by L. Nordentoft and J. Vosmar. Copenhagen: Gyldendal, 1962.
Ariel. 2nd. impression, Copenhagen: Gyldendal, 1964.
"Matador." *Ny nordisk TV dramatik 1965*. Stockholm: Svenska tryckeribolagen, 1965.

Fem Radiospil. Copenhagen: Gyldendal, 1965.
Gyldendals Julebog 1966. Copenhagen: Gyldendal, 1966.
"En halv Alen Vand." *30 Danske Noveller.* Ed. by Charles Haugböll. Copenhagen: Carit Andersens Forlag, 1967.
Tre Skuespil. Copenhagen: Gyldendal, 1968.

WORKS BY BRANNER IN ENGLISH

"A Child and a Mouse." Tr. Evelyn Heepe. *Modern Danish Authors,* eds. Niels Heltberg and E. Heepe. Copenhagen, 1946.
"At the End of August." Tr. Evelyn Heepe. *Swans of the North.* Copenhagen: G. E. C. Gad, n.d. Pp. 35–50.
"At the End of August." Tr. Victoria Nott. *The American-Scandinavian Review,* 54 (1966), 281–87.
"Eva." Tr. Lydia Cranfield. *Adam* (London), 16 (1948), 188 ff.; also in *The Norseman,* 13 (January–February 1955), 55–58.
"In a Little While We Shall Be Gone." Trs. Lida Siboni Hanson and Adda Gentry George. *The American-Scandinavian Review,* 30 (1942), 149–57.
"The Judge." Tr. A. I. Roughton. *Contemporary Danish Plays.* Copenhagen: Gyldendal, 1955. Pp. 495–557.
The Mistress. Tr. A. I. Roughton. New York: New American Library, 1953; *The Riding Master* (same translation), London: Secker and Warburg, 1951.
No Man Knows the Night. Tr. A. I. Roughton. London: Secker and Warburg, 1958.
"The Pipe." Tr. Lydia Cranfield. *The Norseman,* 7 (July–August 1949), 271–79.
"The Three Musketeers." Tr. A. I. Roughton. *Contemporary Danish Prose: An Anthology.* Copenhagen: Gyldendal, 1958. Pp. 270–81.
Two Minutes of Silence. Tr. Vera Lindholm Vance, with an introduction by Richard B. Vowles. Madison: University of Wisconsin Press, 1966.

WORKS ON BRANNER

BLIXEN, KAREN. "H. C. Branner: *Rytteren,*" *Bazar* 1–2, 51–63, 71–94 (1957).
———. *Essays.* Copenhagen: Gyldendal, 1965.
BORGEN, JOHAN. "Profilen: H. C. Branner," *Vinduet* 16, 168–78 (1962).
BRÖNDSTED, MOGENS. "Barnet hos H. C. Branner," *Edda* 59, 111–60 (1959).
——— and SVEN MÖLLER KRISTENSEN. *Danmarks Litteratur.* Copenhagen: Gyldendal, 1963.
FREDERIKSEN, EMIL. *H. C. Branner.* Copenhagen: Gyldendal, 1966.

Selected Bibliography

JOHANSEN, NIELS KAAS. "Rytteren i ny belysning," *Gads danske Magasin* 24, 97–102 (1950).

KRISTENSEN, SVEN MÖLLER. *Digtning og livssyn.* Copenhagen: Gyldendal, 1960.

MADSEN, BÖRGE GEDSÖ. "H. C. Branner: A Modern Humanist." *The American-Scandinavian Review,* 47 (1959), 39–45.

MARKEY, T. L. "H. C. Branner: An Encomium," *Scandinavica* 7.1, 39–52 (1968).

RASMUSSEN, STEEN EILER. "Karen Blixens Rungstedlund." In *Det Danske Akademi 1960–1967.* Copenhagen: G. E. C. Gads Forlag. Pp. 251–318.

Tilbageblik paa 30' erne. 1–2. Copenhagen: Stig Vendelkaers forlag, 1967.

VOSMAR, JÖRN. *H. C. Branner.* Copenhagen: Gyldendal, 1959.

VOWLES, RICHARD B. "Bergman, Branner, and Off-Stage Dying," *Scandinavian Studies* 33, 1–9 (1961).

WAMBERG, NIELS BIRGER. "Lidt om H. C. Branners poetiske rekvisitter," *Ord och Bild* 68, 436–445 (1959).

Index

Aarestrup, Emil, 79
Abell, Kjeld, 90–91, 142
A Doll's House (Henrik Ibsen), 45
Ægteskab: 83–84, 86
A la recherche du temps perdu (Marcel Proust), 97
Also sprach Zarathustra (Friedrich Nietzsche), 124
Andersen, Hans Christian, 81
Angelism: in *Rytteren,* 104
Angst: *See* Anxiety
Angst: analysis of, 94–99; compared with *Trommerne,* 94, 95, 97
Anxiety: as flight from reality, 23, 26; as theme in *Legetöj,* 24; as result of personal conflict, 26; as life giving force, 37, 56–57; as result of inability to perform as an artist, 56–57; death anxiety, 57, 63; Judge Olden as source of, 117; as major theme, 158
Ariel (collection): analysis of, 153–56
Ariel (short story): 154
Arrested development: 26, National Socialism as product of, 30; as major theme in *Legetöj,* 30

Barnet leger ved Stranden: similar motifs in *Eftermaele,* 17, 35; analysis of, 35–50; Freudianism in, 37, 38, 46, 47, 48, 49, 50; compared with *Ingen kender Natten,* 38–39; compared with *Lögneren,* 39; compared with *Natteregn,* 89; compared with *Trommerne,* 93
Beyle, Henri, 41

Bjergene: 92; analysis of, 122–29
Björnson, Björnstjerne, 43
Björnvig, Thorkild, 101
Blixen, Karen, 101–3, 112
Böje, Claus, compared with Glahn, 39; as weak character type, 41–42; compared with Paul Morel, 42
Bogholder Mortensen og Greta Garbo: 20, 22, 25, 34; child playing by the shore image in, 44
Bomholt, Julius, 22
Borgen, Johann, interpretation of *Skibet,* 80; of *Bjergene,* 92; letter from Branner to, 93; 142
Brændte Skibe: 127, 129
Brand (Henrik Ibsen), 19
Branner, Fanny (née Frederiksen), 13
Branner, H. C., childhood and early life, 13–14; as an actor, 13; experience in publishing, 14–15
Branner, Karen (née Moldrup), 14
Bredsdorff, Elias, 74–75
Brix, Hans, 100
Bröndsted, Mogens, 43, 44

Caldwell, Erskine, 75
Characterization: technique of, 158
Character types: commercial type, 138; sterile woman type: Mimi Fleischer as in *Drömmen om en Kvinde,* 52; Katrina as in *De blaa Undulater,* 77; strong (good) woman type: as agent in resolution of anxiety, 26–27; Klara Kvistgaard as, 29, 34, 54; Merete Rude as, 32, 54, 59; Lene as in *Ingen*

181

kender Natten, 141, 157–58; strong male character: in Legetöj, 31–32; Dr. Torsteinson as, 41–42; Hans Egge as, 42; weak male character: in Et Barn og en Mus, 21; Martin Lind as, 29; Claus Böje as, 35, 41–42; analysis of 81; Clemens as, 100

Child in man motif: in Surdejgen, 14; flight from reality as source of, 26; as major theme in Legetöj, 30–31; between lovers, 59–60, 82; voice of crying, 60–62, 139, 157, 174

Christ figure: in Angst, 95; in Rytteren, 107, 111–12; in Söskende, 114–15, 119, 121

Clown figure: in Legetöj, 32; Claus Böje as, 41; discussion of, 111–12; Christ figure as, 111; priest as, 135; use of, 157, 163–64

Cocteau, Jean, 112

Collective novel: in Danish literature, 27; technique of, 28; Legetöj as, 72

Copeau, Jacques, 112

Couples (John Updike), 158

Dæmoner ved Daggry: 94

Death myth: as motif in Et Barn og en Mus, 20–21, 55; in Drömmen om en Kvinde, 58; in Historien om Börge, 68, 69; as major theme, 159

De blaa Undulater: 74; analysis of and comparison with Historien om Börge, 76–77; compared with Skibet, 80–81

Den förste Morgen: 82–83, 86

Der brænder en Ild: 130

De tre Musketerer: 81–82

Die Krise des Humanismus: 130, 172

Digteren og Pigen: 125, 130

Döden varer saa længe: 124, 130; details of publication of, 171

Dons, Aage, 101

Dostoevski, Feodor, 149

Drenge om Foraaret: 81, 86

Dreyer, Erik, 89

Drömmen om en Kvinde: splicing of parallel narrative in, 23; analysis of, 50–63; stream-of-consciousness in, 51–52; compared with Den förste Morgen, 82; compared with Shagpiben, 83

Drömmeren: 19–20; flight from reality in, 23; 25

Dumas, Alexander, 13

Eftermæle: presentation of, 15; criticism of, 17; analysis of, 17–19; similar motifs in Barnet leger ved Stranden, 17, 35, 45; lack of security theme in, 80

Efterspil: 161

Egge, Hans, in Eftermæle as precursor to Barnet leger ved Stranden, 17, 19; compared with Hubert in Rytteren, 110

Eliot, T. S., 136

Elmquist, C. J., 161

En halv Alen Vand: 75, 86–87

En Nytaarsklokke: analysis of, 149–50

Espeseth, Karo, 47

Et Barn og en Mus: 20–22; as a precursor to Historien om Börge, 20, 64; death myth in, 20, 21, 58; 74

Et grædende Barn: 43, 143

Ethical worth: as only permanent value as theme, 29

Et Spil om Kærligheden og Döden: compared with Natteregn, 88; analysis of, 150–53

Existentialism: 56–57, 63

Fear and Trembling (Sören Kierkegaard), 125

Festerne: 20

Finnegan's Wake (James Joyce), 153

Fischer, Leck, 27

Flight from Reality: as a motif in Et Barn og en Mus, 21, 23, 26; in Drömmeren, 23, 25–26; in Iris, 23, 26; Surdejgen, 25; Lördag Aften, 26; Dæmoner ved Daggry, 26; as source of child in man motif, 26;

Index

in *Barnet leger ved Stranden*, 44; in *Historien om Börge*, 70
Flöjtespilleren: 20
Frank, Josef Maria, 22
Frederiksen, Emil, 29, 46, 61, 64, 83, 92, 104, 129, 143
Frederiksen, H. C., 13
Freud, Sigmund (and Freudian, Freudianism), 37, 38, 46, 47, 48, 49, 50, 62, 68, 93, 104, 135
Frye, Northrop, 71, 146

Gerdes, Finn, 89–90
Glimt af mig selv: 13; "dreamer" motif in, 20; *Barnet leger ved Stranden* considered a failure in, 45
God: conception of as father figure, 65, 66, 107, 135; existence of, 63; realization of, 64; Judge Olden as figure of, 112, 114–15
Grænselandet: 87
Grundtvig, N. F. S., 132
Gudme, Anne-Katrine, 21, 23–24

Hamlet figure: Martin Lind as, 29
Hamsun, Knut, 39; influence on Branner, 40
Hannibals Træsko: 22–23, 74
Hans Majæstet: 22, 25
Hansen, Martin A., 39, 99
Hedda Gabler (Henrik Ibsen), 112
Hegel, Georg W. F., 125
Heidegger, Martin, 53
Hellman, Lilian, 19
Hemingway, Ernest, 59, 75, 166
Herdal, Harald, 27
Hertel, Hans, 74, 167
Historien om Börge: and Branner's childhood home, 13; *Et Barn og en Mus* as a precursor to, 20; analysis of, 64–73
Hoel, Sigurd, 45, 50, 59, 89, 142
Hostrup, Jens Christian, 13
Hurwitz, Stephan, 119–20
Hvad er Sandhed?: 22, 162, 163

Ibsen, Henrik, 13, 17, 19, 44, 45, 112, 114, 129, 149

183

Idealism: as central problem in *Legetöj* and *Barnet leger ved Stranden*, 35; vulnerability of the idealist, 44
Images: vision of hope on horizon, 38, 94–96, 169, 172–73; child playing by the shore, 43–44, 153; marital love as cure for loneliness, 84; use of, 94-95; repetition of, 158; lover as a child, 161; poplars as, 161; use of light and dark, 123, 173; being placed in a cellar, 173
Ingeborg: 81
Ingemann, B. H., 132
Ingen kender Natten: compared with *Barnet leger ved Stranden*, 38–39, 90; Tomas compared with narrator in *Trommerne* and *Angst*, 96; waking and sleeping motif in, 110; fragment of, 129–30, 172; analysis of, 131–42; Gabriel as recurrent character type in, 138; *Et grædende Barn* as sketch of Tomas, 143
Iris: 23–25, 74, 77; compared with *Ingeborg*, 81
Isaksen: 15; plot compared with that of *Oluf Höeg's Skæbne*, 20; 25; plot in *Legetöj* as reworking of, 34; 74

James, Henry, 90
Jeg elsker dig: analysis of 146–47
Jeg ved en Fuglerede: 130
Jerndorff, Peter, 13
Johansen, Niels Kaas, 100
John Gabriel Borkman (Henrik Ibsen), 112
Jörgen Stein (Jacob Paludan), 163
Joyce, James, 62, 63, 100
Jung, Carl G., 67, 166

Kafka, Franz, 100, 126, 129
Kameliadamen: 74, 76
Katten: 87
Keats, John, 153
Kierkegaard, Sören, 125

Kirk, Hans, 24; comparison of *Fiskerne* with *Legetöj*, 34; 74
Klitgaard, Mogens, 74
Kristensen, Sven Möller, 56
Kristensen, Tom, 100, 127, 144
Kristiansen, Holger, letter from H. C. Branner to, 14, 46–47, 50, 161, 163, 165
Krog, Helge, 45
Kunstens Uafhængighed: discussion of, 144–46; details of publication of, 175

la Cour, Paul, 47-48
Lagerkvist, Pär, 117
Lawrence, D. H., 42–43, 45, 63
Laxness, Halldor Kiljan, 144
Legetöj: compared with *Isaksen*, 15; *To Minutters Stilhed* as a preparatory exercise to, 17, 23; analysis of, 28–34 allegorical interpretation of, 29
Leg ved Stranden: analysis of, 153–54; compared with *De blaa Undulater* and *Historien om Börge*, 154
Lind, Martin, compared to narrator of *Isaksen*, 15; as exponent of maturation, 28; as weak character type, 29; as Hamlet figure, 29; compared to Claus Böje, 35
Little Match Girl (Hans Christian Andersen), 81
Lördag Aften: 23–24, 26, 74, 75
Lukacs, Georg, 172

Main Street (Sinclair Lewis), 162
Maturation: Martin Lind as exponent of, 28; lack of in *Legetöj*, 30; insistence on, 34; in *Historien om Börge*, 72
Metaphors: adults playing like children (or being childish) in *Legetöj*, 30–31; in *Drömmen om en Kvinde*, 57–58; excessive use of, 72
Michaelis, Karen, 40, 47
Mitchell, P. M., 164
Möbel-Psykose (Jörgen Nielsen), 164

Möller, Kai Friis, 48
Mörket mellem Træerne: 153
Moscow Art Theater, 112
Myth: metaphorical use of, 71–72; Garden of Eden myth as setting, 65, 71-72, 162; in *Rytteren;* Christian mythology in *Söskende*, 115; rising and dying god, 126

Naesgaard, Sigurd, 47–49
Name Symbolism in *Legetöj*, 31; in *Barnet leger ved Stranden*, 41; in *Drömmen om en Kvinde*, 63; in *Ingen kender Natten*, 132, 134; in *Thermopylæ*, 148; in *Puritanerne*, 155; first instance of, 161
Napoleon fixation: 28, 31, 47, 163
Natteregn: 87–89, compared with *Sidst i August*, 88; with *Et Spil om Kærligheden of Döden*, 88; with *Om lidt er vi borte*, 88; with *Barnet leger ved Stranden*, 89; with *Drömmen om en Kvinde*, 89; 169
Nielsen, Jörgen, 164
Nielsen, Peter, 13

Off-stage dying: 68, 110; list of occurrences of, 159
Oluf Höegs Skæbne: 20, 25
Om lidt er vi borte: 74; analysis of, 78–79; theme of, 82, 84; (collection) compared with *To Minutters Stilhed* (collection), 86
O'Neill, Eugene, 19, 147

Pengemagt: 74, 77–78
Personal freedom: 34
Petersen, Ole Hyltoft, 27
Plot: of *Legetöj*, 30; of *Barnet leger ved Stranden*, 35–36; linear progression of, 110; of *Ingen kender Natten*, 131
Point of view: 84
Portrait of the Artist as a Young Man (James Joyce), 97
Prometheus: 15, 25
Puritanerne: analysis of, 154–56;

Index

compared with *De blaa Undulater,* 155; compared with *Drömmen om en Kvinde,* 156

Quest motif: in *Barnet leger ved Stranden,* 38, 42, 43, 44, 99; in *Trommerne,* 93, 98–99; in *Angst,* 98–99; in *Söskende,* 119; for absolute definition of truth and reality, 141

Rasmussen, Steen Eiler, 102
Reality: nexus between words and, 35; attempts at objective view of, 39; quest for, 42; flight from, 44, 158; Claus Böje's confrontation with, 44; as major theme in *Drömmen om en Kvinde,* 51; contrast between an idealized version of and actual appearance of as theme in *Legetöj,* 51; in *Historien om Börge,* 68; individual's confrontation with in *Drömmen om en Kvinde,* 56–57; of death, 57; quest for, 98–99, 141; as verbal key in *Thermopylæ,* 148; absolute view of, 148; definition of, 159; retreat from at time of crisis, 166–67
Reichardt, Konstantin, 165
Röde Heste i Sneen: 82, 86
Rosmersholm (Henrik Ibsen), 44, 45
Rytteren: analysis of, 99–112; critical controversy about, 99, 101; criticized by Karen Blixen, 101–3, 112; mythical form in, 101–3; angelism in, 104; Christ figure in, 107; compared with dramatic version of, 109; hand symbolism in, 110; details of publication of, 170

Samtale med en Klovn: 11–12
Sandemose, Aksel, 45, 47
Saroyan, William, 75
Sartre, Jean Paul, 130
Schaldemose, Peer, 89
Scherfig, Hans, 16, 25, 27, 74, 162
Schyberg, Frederik, 75
Security neurosis: 18, 69, 164

Setting: Kejser stores as a state within a state, 28–30; Garden of Eden myth as, 65, 71–72, 162
Shagpiben: 83; compared with *To Minutters Stilhed,* 84, 86
Shelley, Percy B., 153
Sidst i August: 84–85; compared with *Natteregn,* 88
Sidste Skib: 85–86, 138
Similes: See Metaphors
Sjukos Sjæl: 22, 74
Skibet: 79–81; comparison between Börge in *Historien om Börge* and Johannes, 79; comparison between Katrina in *De blaa Undulator* and Johannes, 80; Johan Borgen's interpretation of, 80
Skrevet i Vand: 156
Social prestige: vacuity of as a theme, 15–16
Social responsibility: dilemma of freedom versus, 34; Claus Böje's acceptance of, 40; discovery of, 96
Söderberg, Hjalmar, 174
Sönderby, Knut, 74, 76
Söskende: 90; analysis of, 112–21; Judge Olden as image of God in, 112
Spögelseshestene (Karen Blixen), 102, 112
Steinbeck, John, 75
Stendal. See Beyle, Henri
Strindberg, August, 64, 157
Strindberg "complex," 36
Style: unreliable narrative, 16; use of direct run-on, 21–22; inner monologue, 29, 52–53, 62, 100; narrative intrusion, 33, 53
Suicide: as escape from reality, 44; attempts to, 36, 69, 162
Surdejgen: 14, 25, 161
Symbol: names as, See Name symbolism; bridge game as, 53–54; hands as, 55, 110, 165; fish as, 57, 166; cathedral as, 54–55, 56, 57, 62, 63, 94; mountains as, 84–85, 123, 124, 125, 126; horse as, 101–2, 106, 108–9; lump of sugar as, 106; divine law as, 114; of Christianity,

115, 118, 140, 148; reiterative use of, 147–48

Technique: splicing of parallel narration, 23, 123, 131; use of inner monologue, 29, 52–53, 62, 100; reshuffling of basic images, 42, 94–95; stream-of-consciousness, 72, 136, 158; narrative control in *Angst* and *Trommerne*, 96–99; as procedure, 131; repetition of scene, 133; of characterization, 158; revelation of character by relation to central incident, 164

The Castle (Franz Kafka), 126, 129, 130

The Family Reunion (T. S. Eliot), 136

The Spoils of Poynton (Henry James), 164

The Trial (Franz Kafka), 126, 129, 130

The Wild Duck (Henrik Ibsen), 44, 45

Thermopylæ: analysis of, 147–49

To Minutters Stilhed (short story): 15–16; as preparatory exercise to *Legetöj*, 17; (collection), 75, 79; later version of, 84; compared with *Natteregn*, 87; (collection) translation of, 90; earlier version of, 161–62

Transformation of character: through agency of good woman, 26, 89; of Martin Lind, 32; Merete Rude as capable of effecting, 58; of Susanne in *Rytteren*, 106; through individuation and maturation, 72; after hearing the cry of a child, 139; of Tomas in *Ingen kender Natten*, 142

Tre Mænd vender Hjem: 24–25

Troilus and Cressida (William Shakespeare), 101, 151

Trommerne: 90; analysis of, 92–94; comparison with *Barnet leger ved Stranden*, 93; comparison with *Angst*, 94, 95, 97

Updike, John, 158

Vandring langs Floden: 128–30, 143–44

Vesaas, Tarjei, 66, 128

Vosmar, Jörn, 22, 35, 42, 45, 46, 64, 83, 99, 110, 123, 129, 136

Wahl, Einar, as precursor to Dr. Torsteinson, 17–18

Wedekind, Frank, 82

Wimmer, August, 48

Woolf, Virginia, 62, 63

DATE DUE